GALVESTON'S
MACEO
FAMILY
EMPIRE

....

BOOTLEGGING &
THE BALINESE ROOM

*T. Nicole Boatman, Scott H. Belshaw
& Richard B. McCaslin*

THE
History
PRESS

Published by The History Press
Charleston, SC 29403
www.historypress.net

Copyright © 2014 by T. Nicole Boatman, Scott H. Belshaw and
Richard B. McCaslin
All rights reserved

First published 2014

Manufactured in the United States

ISBN 978.1.62619.753.4

Library of Congress Control Number: 2014953188

CONTENTS

ACKNOWLEDGEMENTS

I want to acknowledge the love and support of my family and friends. Specifically, Mom and Dad, you guys have always given me the necessary strength and confidence for school, as well as for this particular project. You guys have reassuringly coached me through the many obstacles with which I have been faced. Also, Granny and Papa, you guys believed in me more than I believed in myself sometimes, and a special thanks for your help when I lived like a vagabond, jumping between classes and work. Your hearty breakfasts got me through many long days. Finally, to the ladies in my life who have listened to me moan and groan and reminded me why this work was so important to finish: Abi, Alison, Ashley and Sarah Bear. I wouldn't have made it through these past two years without your encouragement and our frequent nights at Cheers.

I would also like to express my very great appreciation to Dr. Chad Trulson for his assistance on this project. Before the birth of this project, you graded me harder than any professor, but it made me a better writer. I acknowledge the time you put into this project during its early stages. Also, I am grateful for the suggestions and constructive criticism you provided, which ultimately made it a stronger thesis. In addition, I would like to thank Rosenberg Library, Moore Memorial Public Library, University of Houston's M.D. Anderson Library and University of Texas Dolph Briscoe Center for American History for your assistance in my research efforts. Thank you Amanda Belshaw for your help with the photos. Lastly, and most importantly, I would like to thank Dr. Scott Belshaw and Dr. Richard McCaslin, who collaborated with me on each step of this project. It has been great working with you guys!

–NB

I want to acknowledge the assistance of my wife, Amanda, the love of my life. Your assistance on this project was greatly appreciated. I also want to thank my father-in-law, Warren Burl Leeson; God rest his soul. When I joined the family, I heard his great stories regarding the bootlegging families and the mafia in Galveston. That inspired me to dig deeper into the history of Galveston. I enjoyed hearing his stories of going to the Balinese Room in the 1940s. Thanks, Dad. I want to thank all my Clear Lake peeps for the encouragement on this project. Having grown up on the Texas Gulf Coast, I was exposed to its rich history and fun people. Go Falcons. I want to thank my kids for striving to be the best at everything they do. They are the true meaning of what love is.

–SHB

I simply want to thank my colleagues Scott Belshaw and Nicole Boatman for including me in this project. It is one of the great joys in academia that we get the opportunity to learn new things all the time. This project is a perfect example. And I of course want to thank my wife, Jana McCaslin, for allowing me to continue playing in this sandbox.

–RBM

INTRODUCTION

Texas history is fascinating because of the many kinds of people who have settled in the Lone Star State. No matter what variety of folks you encounter elsewhere in the United States, it seems you also find them living somewhere in Texas. Texans, of course, celebrate their diverse ethnic heritage in festivals and other events that commemorate the immigrants who arrived from six of the seven continents on Earth. If a substantial number of people had ever emigrated from Antarctica, Texans are certain the best of them would have landed in their state, too.

But memory, especially public memory, is selective. Through time, and the hard work of many opinion shapers of all sorts, Texans have embraced popular images that reflect what most of them think the people of their state are really like. Arguably, the cowboy and the oilman are at the top of the list, followed by everyone from cowgirls to outlaws. All of these are also accepted by the outside world as the faces of Texas. But the fact that there were gangsters in the Lone Star State seems to be almost completely overlooked in published histories. And Texas became the home of not just any mafioso, but real Sicilian-born mobsters who built an empire in the island city of Galveston during the first half of the twentieth century.

Salvatore "Sam" Maceo and Rosario "Rose" Maceo are an integral part of the Texas story. They came to America looking for opportunity, and like many other immigrants, they found it in Texas. Unfortunately for their public legacy, they made a fortune in illicit enterprises such as bootlegging, gambling and prostitution. Drawing heavily on the example of the criminal organizations they encountered in their native Sicily, they carefully cultivated the goodwill of their neighbors in Galveston by sharing the profits of their operations, and in turn, most local residents generally condoned their activities. Certainly the Maceo brothers were no saints, but it can be argued that they played a crucial role in bringing prosperity to Galveston after it had endured a century of turmoil and tragedy.

This book on the "Island Empire" of the Maceos thus brings attention to an overlooked piece of Texas history, as well as the story of the United States. It is important to understand all aspects of the impact of European immigration on both the state and the nation and to understand that the positive and negative impacts were not just confined to one region. The insights into organized crime in Galveston that are offered in this study of the Maceos should prove useful to scholars seeking to understand its development in other cities. It is certainly intriguing to discover the role played by the brothers in the rise of Las Vegas, as well as their family's continuing influence there. Perhaps the irony of how Las Vegas prospered through the same activities for which the Maceos were prosecuted will not escape the notice of the careful reader.

RICHARD B. McCASLIN, PHD
University of North Texas

1

ISLAND EMPIRE

GALVESTON AND THE MACEOS

S ince the beginning of the 1900s, organized crime families have played a significant role in American society. However, organized crime groups are not a modern invention, nor are they unique to the United States. Such groups have been around for centuries, and they can be found throughout multiple cultural groups. What most Americans consider to be organized crime is synonymous with the term "mafia." It has been argued that the terms "mafia" and "La Cosa Nostra" did not come into use until the middle of the twentieth century. Nevertheless, while these terms may not have been in use prior to that point in time, the criminal activities that are associated with these types of groups had already proven to be prevalent in many different locations.

The American mafia can be traced back to the southern Italian island of Sicily. In general, it began as a response to the oppression and legal insecurities perpetuated by outside governments in southern Italy. There were various foreign leaders who took control of the area prior to the twentieth century. Typically, these foreign rulers failed to meet the needs of Sicilians. As a result, landowners reached out to criminal groups, who promised to protect their land and assets. Over time, these groups received compensation from the elite groups for the services they provided. They also received support from local churches because even the religious leaders recognized the good these groups brought to their communities.[1]

When a large influx of immigrants from Sicily arrived in North American port cities in the late nineteenth century, they brought with them their history of organized crime. When faced with the same social and financial disabilities as they had experienced in their past location, they resorted to similar organized activities. As historian Stephen L. Mallory has explained, many major American cities suffered from unemployment and overcrowding due to extremely high numbers of incoming Europeans. These conditions forced Sicilians back into their old business of organized crime. In fact, Mallory goes so far as to assert that all organized crime with Italian roots in the United States, which is commonly referred to as mafia activity, can be traced back to Sicily.[2]

Although organized crime is not limited to port cities, these locations were largely associated with crime families at the turn of the twentieth century due to the high number of immigrants entering such communities. New York and New Orleans were among the communities that endured the most organized crime.[3] Yet while organized crime families also infamously controlled inland cities such as Chicago, smaller port cities like Galveston were among those greatly affected by the incoming crime families. Because of its high numbers of European immigrants, Galveston was sometimes referred to as the "Ellis Island of the West," a distinction that had both good and bad perspectives.[4]

Galveston is and has been a unique city in Texas. Today, it appears to be nothing more than a tourist destination, popular for weekend getaways. However, the city has a rich history dating back to the landing of the first European explorers. The many inhabitants of the island have experienced the highs and lows of living on a tiny island. Galveston Island lies exposed to the fury of Mother Nature, a fact that has cost the town millions of dollars, as well as thousands of lives. At the same time, the island's isolation from the mainland has proven to have its advantages. This detail led to some of the island's most exciting years.

As local writer Paul Burka has explained, the city of Galveston stands on an island that is little more than a long sandbar. This meant that the island residents were not protected from the ocean's surge or the storms that rolled in from the sea. This was unique in the fact that no other port city in the United States was established on a sandbar island, probably because of the risks such a location would pose. Instead, sandbar islands have frequently hosted resort cities, such as Miami Beach and Atlantic City.[5] Nevertheless, Galveston was considered to be an ideal natural harbor, and it attracted early attention as a port site. During the early 1800s, the island was settled and named while Texas was still a territory of Mexico. Shortly afterward, it came under the control of the Republic of Texas.[6]

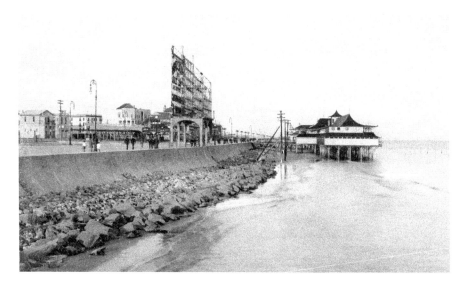

Bathhouses lined the Seawall throughout Galveston's "Open Era." They served as a tourist attraction for the city. *Courtesy of the Rosenberg Library.*

After being officially chartered as a city in 1838, Galveston quickly made a name for itself as a port. Between 1838 and 1860, ten wharves were established on the island. The island's importance as a port was already proving to be the strongest economic asset for the new city. As historians Patricia B. Bixel and Elizabeth H. Turner recall, the island community's only concern was a couple of sandbars, which created obstacles for ships coming to and leaving the port. However, after Galveston's Deep Water Committee allied with the United States Army Corps of Engineers in 1889, the harbor was deepened, alleviating the problem. By 1899, "Galveston port ranked second in the country in cotton exports, third in wheat, sixth in cattle, seventh in corn, and thirteenth in flour."[7]

By the end of the nineteenth century, Galveston could claim to be the most modern city in the state of Texas. More than that, it was considered to be one of the most developed trade centers from New Orleans to San Francisco.[8] Some called Galveston the "Seaport of the West."[9] Because of its continued growth into the twentieth century, others referred to Galveston as the "Wall Street of the Southwest."[10] Again, as discussed earlier, still others referred to Galveston Island as the "Ellis Island of the West" due to the strong flow of immigrants into and through the city during the first couple decades of the twentieth century. According to writer Susan W. Hardwick, the *New York Herald* even named Galveston as the "New York of the Gulf."[11]

These various nicknames and the reputation that Galveston held were due to several factors. As frequently noted by proud locals, Galveston was the location for many firsts in Texas. These included the first electric lights, first opera house, first telephone, first hospital, first golf course, first country club, first YMCA and first law firm. The list goes on. In addition to the quick

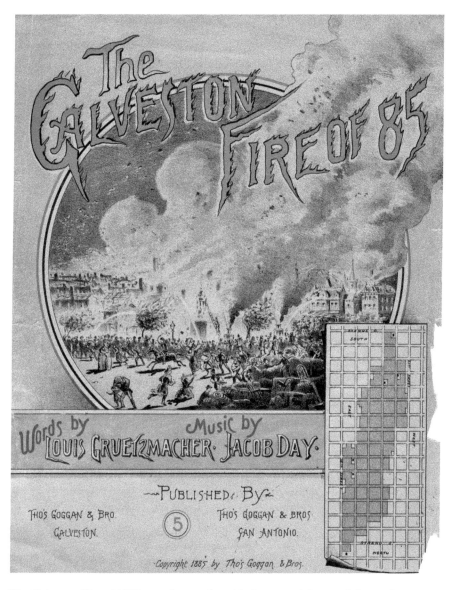

The Galveston Fire of 1885 spread over a forty-block area and destroyed almost six hundred buildings and homes. *Courtesy of the Rosenberg Library.*

economic development on the island, the city became a cultural center.[12] This cultural vitality was largely due to the growing immigrant population. Thanks to many of the immigrants, Galveston had theaters and operas when other Texas cities were simply trying to fight Indians and pave their roads.[13]

In addition to the cultural activity introduced by these immigrants, Galveston's population also developed a high level of tolerance for vice. In fact, Galveston had a long history of transient populations and diverse groups that contributed to this tolerance for illicit activities. As seen in many culturally diverse communities, this translated into a greater acceptance of activities that were not regarded by residents as innately wrong but merely wrong because of local, state or national laws. Of course, the immigrants were not solely responsible for this tolerance.

The tolerance was further perpetuated by the impact of many tragedies that Galvestonians suffered prior to the twentieth century. There were several horrific hurricanes that hit the sandbar city during the 1800s.[14] Plus, Galveston suffered many yellow fever outbreaks throughout the same time period.[15] In 1885, the community was swept by a large fire that destroyed over forty blocks. Then, in 1900, the island experienced its greatest disaster yet, the Great Storm of 1900.[16]

To date, the Great Storm of 1900 is considered the deadliest natural disaster to ever hit the United States.[17] This hurricane hit Galveston early in September and wiped out a large percentage of the population; some estimated as much as one-fifth of the island's populace died. In the aftermath, progressive city leaders not only cleaned up the widespread destruction but also developed a plan to protect residents from future marine disasters. This is what led to the building of one of the greatest seawalls ever constructed in the world. Furthermore, the island underwent the remarkable process of raising the overall elevation, known as a grade raise.[18]

After so much tragedy and so many obstacles, and despite the hard work of many locals, Galveston fell from its lofty status as one of the largest and most prosperous cities in Texas. Many residents became involved in rebuilding their island city, but some did not feel it was worth the risk. There was a large migration off the island and onto the mainland in the early years of the twentieth century. The locals remained focused on recovering from the Great Storm of 1900, but outside investors and corporations were reluctant to settle businesses on an island that had proven to be in the path of such overwhelming destruction. Although the island community continued to operate as a port city, by 1920, Galveston had fallen behind many other cities such as Houston, whose leaders had deepened its

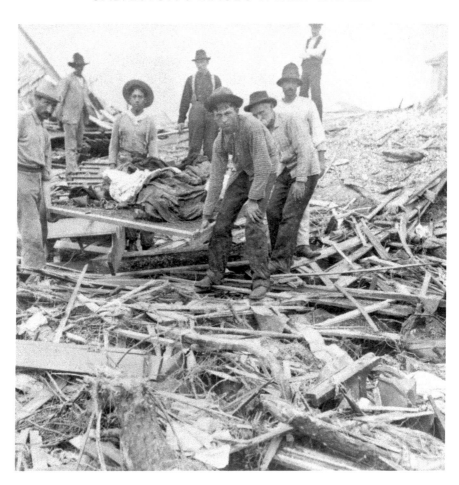

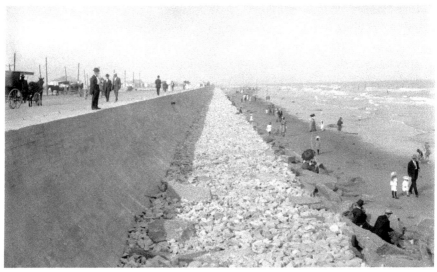

harbor. The economic decline experienced on the island set in motion the city's transition toward tourism, despite many locals' reluctance and overall distaste for such business.[19]

This move toward tourism also pushed Galvestonians further into an already existing underworld. As explained earlier, vice crimes were not novel ideas to many of the locals in Galveston. As Robert Nieman has discussed, Galveston developed some of the highest rates of prostitution for a city in Texas, "with over 1,000 working hookers" and a "ratio of 1 prostitute for every 62 citizens."[20] Gambling, liquor and prostitution were technically illegal. However, all three activities were not only tolerated by the citizens of Galveston but also allowed by the city officials, who "endorsed the idea of an open, but clean town."[21]

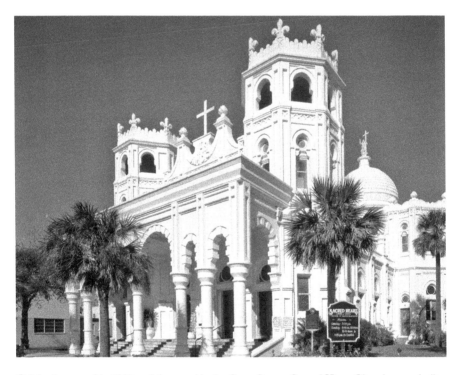

Originally erected in 1884 and destroyed in the Great Storm, Sacred Heart Church was rebuilt in 1904 and included two original stained-glass windows. *Courtesy of the Library of Congress.*

Opposite, top: The Great Storm of 1900 remains the deadliest natural disaster in American history, killing an estimated one-fifth of Galveston's population. *Courtesy of the Library of Congress.*

Opposite, bottom: Pictured is the Seawall and beach of Galveston after construction of the wall and the grade raising, both precautions against future hurricanes. *Courtesy of the Library of Congress.*

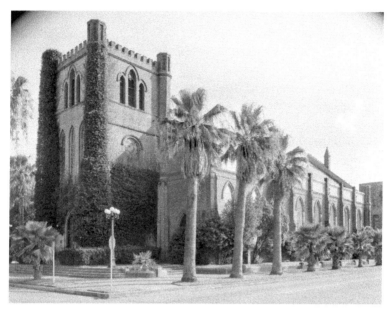

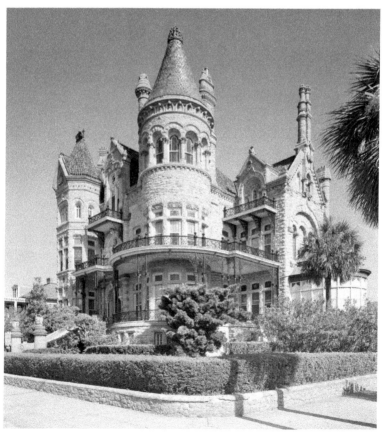

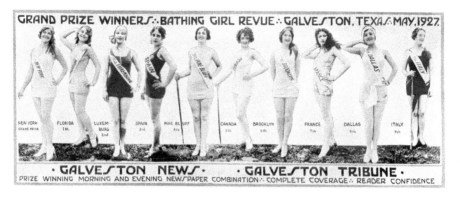

The Galveston Island Bathing Girl Revue was the first international beauty contest. The Maceo brothers served as the main pageant sponsors. *Courtesy of the Rosenberg Library.*

Opposite, top: The Trinity Episcopal Church of Galveston was constructed in 1857 and survived the Great Storm of 1900. *Courtesy of the Library of Congress.*

Opposite, bottom: Built in 1892, the Bishop's Palace, or Gresham's Castle, survived the Great Storm. The building is located at Fourteenth and Broadway. *Courtesy of the Library of Congress.*

Ironically, during the same time that Galveston was making its transition into tourism, the federal government was enacting the Volstead Act, which banned the production, importation and consumption of alcoholic beverages in the United States.[22] This federal legislation unintentionally pushed the island community toward more vice. The geographic attributes of Galveston, especially its fine port, made it a popular location for smuggling illegal liquor into the United States. The two new trades—tourism and bootlegging—complemented each other. The availability of liquor on the island encouraged tourism. Likewise, tourism increased the demand for the growth and expansion of Galveston's illicit trade in alcohol. Thus, both vice and tourism increased, and Galveston's underworld offered new opportunities for anyone interested in making an illegal profit.

The port city's move toward more vice crime created more wealth for all of its residents. There clubs were open all year round, providing jobs for the residents. As stated above, the popularity of gambling and other entertainment combined with the availability of alcohol to attract even more tourists. Plus, such activities pulled in more visitors all year, whereas the beach activities attracted tourists only during the warmest months. Overall, the underworld activities on the island promoted greater financial stability in Galveston and provided a pathway to financial recovery.

About this time, Galveston welcomed a new family on the rise. The Maceos arrived in Galveston around 1910. Originally from Sicily, the family immigrated to New Orleans at the turn of the twentieth century. Like many Italians before and after them, the Maceos left their native country in search of greater opportunities and security while avoiding further economic and governmental oppression.[23] Shortly after settling in Louisiana, they relocated to the Texas Gulf Coast in hopes of greater financial security. Salvatore and Rosario were the two brothers from the family who originally came to Galveston, working as barbers.[24] The rest of the family followed the two men shortly afterward.

Rosario, known as Rose, and Salvatore, known as Sam, quickly became involved in Galveston's vice activity. Rose would become notorious as the

BELOW: Photographer catches a few of the many who attended Galveston's big Mardi Gras Dance. Left to right: Mrs. Frank Maceo and Vic Maceo; Mrs. and Mr. Anthony Fertitta; Mrs. and Mr. Rose Maceo.

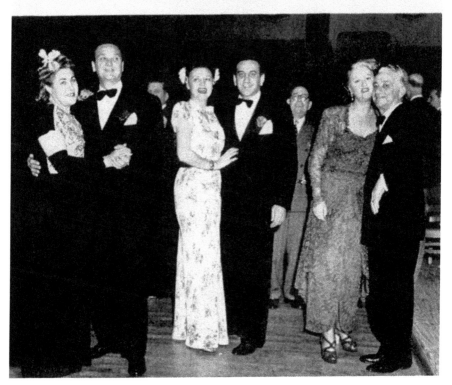

Courtesy of the Rosenberg Library.

enforcer of the family, playing an important role in their operations. However, just as he provided protection to the crime family, Rose also provided the locals with an informal police force, much like his mafia predecessors had done in Sicily. Rose's men regularly patrolled the island's streets, especially at night. It was reported that his regulation of activity led to some of the island's lowest rates of crime, at least in areas not of interest to the Maceo family. Overall, Rose was a feared yet respected man in the community.

Sam, on the other hand, became the front man and the public image of the family. In addition to being favorably mentioned in various newspapers and magazines across the nation, he was also an active philanthropist outside the limelight. There are numerous reports of Sam providing others with that which they lacked. This included individual Galvestonians who needed loans, as well as local charities and churches.

The two men began with bootlegging during the Prohibition era and quickly progressed to the top of the Galveston underworld. Even after Prohibition was repealed, the Maceo brothers expanded their businesses exponentially, including first-class clubs that offered gambling, alcohol and top entertainers from all over the country.[25] From the early 1920s

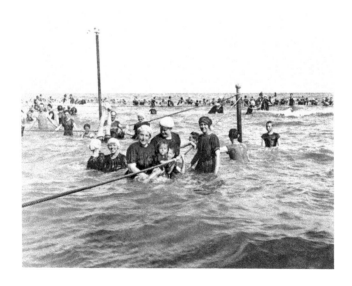

Bathing in the Gulf of Mexico in Galveston, Texas. Galveston's setting naturally attracted pleasure-seekers. *Courtesy of the Library of Congress.*

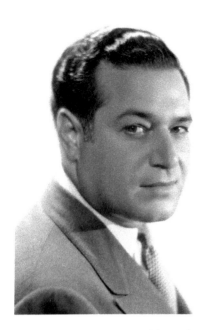

Sam Maceo, known as an activist and philanthropist to locals, opened a number of popular clubs and restaurants in Galveston County. *Courtesy of the Rosenberg Library.*

until the 1950s, Rose and Sam built an empire in Galveston. The establishments they built on the island were one of a kind, and the Maceo name became nationally recognized during the following decades.

The Maceos, of course, were not the only well-known underworld leaders during this time. Despite the illegality of gambling, prostitution and alcohol throughout Prohibition, similar operations were fairly common, especially throughout the Roaring Twenties. Interestingly, though, Sam and Rose Maceo kept their businesses afloat for more than thirty years, long after many of their contemporaries had died, been arrested or retired. They progressed through the hierarchy of the island city's underworld relatively quickly, and they operated without much pressure from law enforcement for more than three decades. These facts are particularly of interest.

How did Sam and Rose Maceo gain so much power in so little time? What factors influenced the brothers' rapid progression to the top of Galveston's underworld? How did they stay in that position for so long? In the case of the Maceos, it is important to not just review the surrounding social circumstances throughout the brothers' reign but also to outline Galveston's and Sicily's histories prior to the Maceo family's arrival in the United States. The history of the two island communities, as well as the conditions resulting from historical events, provided the two Maceo brothers with the perfect opportunity to become illicit entrepreneurs. At the same time, the financial resources the brothers provided to Galvestonians in return remedied the setbacks of Galveston's past, which contributed to local tolerance.

The current literature on the Maceos fails to explain the brothers' success throughout the three decades. Although historians and journalists have previously discussed the Maceo family and their activities on the island, the discussions are generally included within a broader historical account of Galveston.[26] To these historians, it appears the Maceos played only a minor role in the history of the community. On the contrary, the Maceos' arrival in the small Gulf Coast port had a lasting impact, not just on Galveston, but also on organized crime outside of the island. The following pages will outline the Maceos' years spent in Galveston and the influence they had on others.

The success of Sam and Rose can be partially, but not wholly, explained by a combination of their Sicilian heritage, their experiences upon arriving in America and the history of Galveston, as discussed above. Together, these various social factors and personal qualities essentially prepared the brothers for success, giving them all of the necessary tools to become involved in the island city's organized crime and to build an empire within it. These factors, along with the brothers' agreeable natures and the instability of existing gangs, are what determined the success of their empire-building efforts.

Essentially, Sam and Rose Maceo landed on Galveston Island with the skills and knowledge to become involved in its preexisting vice activities. More than that, they were well liked and settled in a region where citizens freely accepted vice and the rackets that came with it. Galvestonians had already suffered many horrible events. Then, Sam and Rose provided the island with entertainment and contributed to making the city a wealthy community once again. In turn, this proved to be somewhat therapeutic to the residents of such a broken community.

The following chapters will outline these various factors and attempt to explain just how each element helped to form the ideal circumstances for an organized crime family, or mafia. The Maceos' remarkable success was largely due to the instability in the island city, but it also came because of what the Maceo brothers had to offer and how they approached the opportunity in front of them. It is possible that had another crime family invaded Galveston, they would not have been met with such acceptance and tolerance. That is what makes the Maceo family unique in the history of the American mafia.

It should not be overlooked in considering their success that the Maceo brothers introduced establishments such as the Hollywood Dinner Club and the infamous Balinese Room. The Hollywood Dinner Club was an antecedent to the Balinese Room, but both locations were described as exquisitely decorated. Nothing but the best was allowed in either location. The Balinese Room was known for its luxurious décor, fine dining and first-class entertainment. This particular location came to be on the Texas Rangers

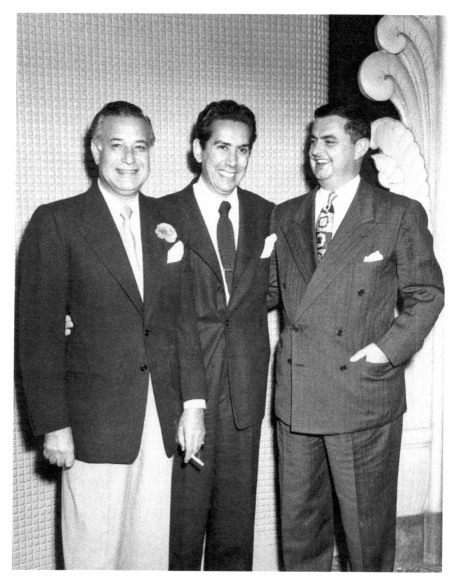

From left: Sam Maceo; famed pianist Carmen Cavallaro; and Mayor Herbie Cartwright, an alleged advocate of the brothers' rackets. *Courtesy of the Rosenberg Library.*

and state officials' radar due to its reputation statewide, and it became the target of the investigations that finally brought the Maceo family's activities to a halt.

The demise of Sam and Rose Maceo and the downfall of their island empire will be analyzed in the final chapter. But the brothers began something

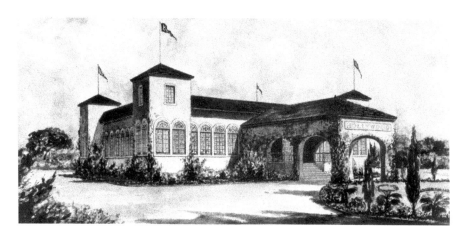

The Hollywood Dinner Club was the Maceos' first club. Later, the Texas Rangers located over $1 million in gambling paraphernalia at the club. *Courtesy of the Rosenberg Library.*

unique during their time in Galveston. It appears that other crime families showed interest in their activities. Shortly after they established their name, other locations began to offer similar entertainment. Since then, criminal organizations have experienced exponential growth under the roofs of such businesses, as seen in places such as Las Vegas. Therefore, it seems the Maceo brothers not only had a positive influence on Galvestonians and the island's economy but also on the expansion of other cities with similar venues, such as Las Vegas, where members of the Maceos' extended family continue to operate today.

SETTING THE STAGE

TURBULENT HISTORY OF GALVESTON ISLAND

When people generally think of the mafia in the United States, they think of the legendary five families of New York or the terror Al Capone inflicted on Chicago in the 1920s. Organized crime is not typically associated with Galveston, Texas. Yet the city has a rich history that includes a popular crime syndicate that operated on the island for over three decades. Today, the island is little more than a small tourist location along the Gulf Coast of Texas—just a ghost of its exciting past. In fact, as of 2010, the United States Census Bureau reported that Galveston Island had just under forty-eight thousand residents.[27] This number is actually down from when the city peaked in the middle of the twentieth century, during the later years of the Maceo family operations.

According to the most current census, the largest number of citizens claim to work in healthcare or education agencies. This is not surprising considering the University of Texas Medical Branch is located within the city. The next largest group claims to be involved in "arts, entertainment, and recreation, and accommodation and food services."[28] This is largely reflective of the economy of the modern island city, which survives primarily as a tourist location. Locals dislike the reliance on tourism and feel that Galveston should focus greater attention on the city's port activities.[29] Nevertheless, the tourism industry provides a stable economy for the island's workers, as it did for most of the past century.

Furthermore, roughly 30 percent of Galveston's current population declared that they were Hispanic or Latino, and 46 percent reported that they were white. Just under 15 percent of the population claimed to be born outside the United States. However, one can still get a glimpse of the island's complex history when looking at the current residents' reported ancestry. The Census Bureau reported that 10 percent of the population is of German descent, 8 percent is Irish in origin, almost 7 percent is of English descent and 5 percent have Italian ancestry.[30] This clearly recalls the days when Galveston was the "Ellis Island of the West" and welcomed many immigrants, including the Maceo family from Sicily.[31]

For such a small and seemingly ordinary town, Galveston has an extremely rich history that provides a stage for the activities of a powerful crime family: the Maceos. The island's past involvement in organized crime is largely due to the significant number of European immigrants who chose to settle in Galveston. The Maceos were among those immigrants, and the empire they built throughout the first half of the twentieth century was impressive on many different levels. While the Maceo family, led by brothers Sam and Rose, ran rackets in the island city that were essentially ignored or even condoned by leaders, state and federal officials often spent their time investigating other more famous members of the American mafia.

Sam and Rose Maceo dominated Galveston from the 1920s to the 1950s. During these years, Galveston gained the reputation of being an "open city" due to its many illegal activities, as well as the island community's long-standing tolerance for such operations.[32] Although this reputation was largely due to the Maceos' efforts, the seeds had already been planted many years earlier for the two brothers to successfully dominate the island city's underworld.

Almost since the arrival of Galveston's first settlers, vice crime has existed on the small stretch of land; such activities are deeply rooted in the island's history. Therefore, in order to understand why the brothers were able to establish and then continue their operations without interruption for as long as they did, it is necessary to review the history of Galveston. The history of the island city created the perfect conditions for the Maceos' success. Without such conditions, local residents, city officials and law enforcement officers would not have tolerated the Maceo family's illicit operations.

The inhabitants of Galveston have long had a remarkable tolerance for vice activities. These inhabitants have largely been of a transient nature—nomadic Karankawa Indians in the early years, followed by pirates, then Civil War soldiers and a postbellum flood of immigrants. Although a stable group of locals persisted after the establishment of the city, additional immigrants continued to ebb in and out of Galveston's social scene. What resulted from this type of population was a high tolerance for illicit activities and an attitude of free will. Overall, this population seems to have created a large moral gray area that favored the Maceo family's activities.

In addition to hosting an ever-changing multitude of ethnic groups, Galveston also suffered many turbulent events. These events played a role in hindering Galveston's potential growth. Galveston was the largest city in the state of Texas from 1850 until 1890.[33] However, in its early years, the island suffered two significant yellow fever epidemics. In addition, the island also endured several natural disasters. In fact, by 1890, Galveston had already overcome many hurricanes, as well as a terrible fire in 1885.[34] Then, only fifteen years after the fire, Galveston endured the most deadly natural disaster in the history of the United States.[35] These events had a lasting impact on the state of the island, restricting the growth of legitimate commerce and pushing many local residents to seek more illicit ways to make money.

The Great Storm of 1900 killed a large portion of Galveston's population. Among the survivors, a large percentage chose to leave the island instead of rebuild. This resulted in an even greater instability within the island's economy. Furthermore, some outsiders even began to view Galveston as a liability. Companies were reluctant to settle on the small island. Although the island's economy had not completely collapsed, people believed that it soon would. Unless the island city benefited from a new source of income, Galveston would be faced with an unavoidable expiration date. Luckily, money is exactly what the Maceo family provided.

Gambling, prostitution and alcohol had already become commonplace vices on Galveston Island before Sam and Rose Maceo arrived. Thus, when the brothers emerged, they did not introduce novel ideas to the residents. Instead, they merely focused and organized the previously established activities—in other words, the Maceos took advantage of Galveston's predisposition for vice. Plus, Sam and Rose expanded on these existing activities. To their great advantage, the previous tragedies endured by Galvestonians, as well as the diverse population of the island, seem to have cultivated an environment fertile for the businesses introduced by the two brothers.

Sam and Rose operated many businesses on the island. Their first major establishment was the Hollywood Dinner Club. This location allowed the brothers to dabble with new ideas. For example, the club was the first of its kind, offering gambling, alcohol (even during Prohibition), fine dining and top entertainment. However, it was not until the Maceo brothers opened the Balinese Room years later that they perfected the original idea behind the Hollywood Dinner Club. The Balinese Room quickly became a nationally recognized operation and was a major reason for the success of Sam and Rose, as well as the Maceo family's downfall in the 1950s.

Although not everyone participated firsthand in the brothers' illicit businesses, most of the residents of Galveston endorsed their activities. The citizens recognized that such unlawful activities benefited Galveston's economy. There were jobs for everyone. Large loans were being provided by local banks. Some city officials and law enforcement officers were receiving money, through payoffs or bribes, which helped to inflate the local budget.[36] As a bonus, gambling, prostitution and drinking, especially during the Prohibition era, attracted people from all over. These activities became the focus of the island's revitalized tourism industry.

This focus on tourism became an important reason for the city to turn a blind eye to illegal activities. After so much destruction in one city, the locals understood that they had few choices other than to accept tourists as a major economic asset. They also understood that the island's vice activities promoted tourism. Fortunately for the Maceos, Galveston was essentially isolated from the rest of the state, so there was little interference from outside officials. For many years, the only real authority on the island came from local law enforcement, and its members fully understood the benefit of not interfering with the Maceo family.

Much like the general population in Galveston, the chief of police and the sheriff in Galveston County both seem to have recognized the economic benefits of the Maceos' businesses. Both of these men avoided interfering with Maceo operations. There is also evidence that suggests other city officials participated in this tolerance.[37] As stated, there was not a lot of outside attention. Since the island city's own leading law enforcement officers elected not to confront the brothers, Sam and Rose continued their operations until state and, later, federal agencies took notice and intervened.

GALVESTON'S EARLY HETEROGENEOUS SETTLERS

As mentioned, Galveston was settled largely by transient populations. This particular pattern started even before European explorers discovered the island. The first known inhabitants were nomadic Karankawa Indians. Then, after the arrival of the Europeans, the island experienced an influx of other transient groups, including pirates, Civil War soldiers and sailors and immigrants from outside the United States. Each subsequent group, having a different background, brought new ideals and cultural practices to the island city. In the end, Galveston, like many port cities, was significantly more heterogeneous than more insulated inland locations.

The earliest known inhabitants on Galveston Island were the Karankawa Indians. These natives understood the island was at the mercy of the sea. Therefore, the tribe primarily used the area for hunting and gathering, while settling on the safer mainland.[38] The group's first encounter with European immigrants occurred in 1528, when a group of Spaniards washed ashore. Álvar Núñez Cabeza de Vaca led these men. He described the natives as delighted to help his shipwrecked crew. The Indians led the explorers from the wreckage to their own village, with fires placed at regular intervals to ensure the Spaniards did not suffer from the cold.[39]

Immediately after their exile, the survivors learned that some crew members had perished with the ship. Even worse, after enduring a harsh winter with the Karankawas, only five Spaniards remained alive. In addition to the deaths experienced among the lost explorers, the Karankawas' numbers were greatly depleted. The natives were plagued by disease, which they were rightfully convinced had come from the new arrivals. By the end of the winter season, the disease had wiped out half the original village.[40] Despite these hardships, and potential conflict, the explorers remained with the Karankawas for six more years before relocating to Mexico. The Karankawas did not encounter another group of Europeans until 1685.[41]

The Karankawas are also thought to have been cannibals. Journalist Gary Cartwright argued that the Karankawas, like other tribes in the region, believed that consuming their enemies gave them greater strength. Historian David G. McComb shared the story of a young woman who encountered and studied the Karankawa people during these early years. Local historian Alice W. Oliver claimed that the adult Karankawas applied blue paint to their faces, which commonly represented participation in cannibalism. However, other historians claim that it was not the natives who partook in cannibalism but the Spaniards. As Charles W. Hayes explained, after enduring an especially harsh winter, the Spaniards were forced to eat their own men. Reportedly, not only were the Karankawas not cannibals, but the Indians were also horrified by the occurrence, given their compassion and respect for human life.[42]

Thus, there are indications that either group could have been guilty of this ghastly behavior. Whether the Karankawas or the Spaniards participated in cannibalism is uncertain. Nevertheless, it does appear that cannibalism occurred on Galveston Island. It seems important to consider that one of mankind's most taboo practices occurred during the earliest years of the island. From its inception, the island's location and lack of resources fostered ideals and values that were not found in other cultures and times, and the local environment seemed to encourage practices that were prohibited elsewhere.

In addition, the Karankawas represent the first transient group on the island. This tribe lived as nomads—hunting and gathering in various regions throughout the four seasons.[43] Furthermore, the Spaniards, the next transients, were among the first to leave an impression on the region before relocating to a new location. As mentioned, Cabeza de Vaca and his men spent six years on the island before moving south to Mexico, and during that time, more than half the Karankawas died. It appears likely that this is the mark that group left on the island, and it is not a positive one. Likewise, each subsequent group that arrived on the island left a mark in Galveston's history, and the results were not always good.

The next group to arrive were Frenchmen led by Robert de La Salle. However, it was Louis-Michel Aury who erected the first French settlement on the island in 1816. His establishment was not merely populated by Frenchmen but also Haitians. The group brought with them a large collection of stolen Spanish treasures. When Aury moved farther inland to aid in the war for Mexican independence, two French brothers, Jean and Pierre Lafitte, took command. Jean Lafitte, in particular, invested in Galveston. He constructed numerous buildings and established about one thousand settlers in a village he called Campeachy.[44]

Despite the development on the island subsequent to Lafitte's arrival, the new leader participated in his own dishonest activities. Jean Lafitte was a notorious pirate. He used Galveston as a base for illegal operations, using the bay to capture ships and then selling stolen merchandise in New Orleans, from where he had been expelled by United States officials, and at ports along the Mississippi River.[45] Galveston provided the perfect location for such business. As explained by McComb, "Claimed by the United States, Mexico, and Spain, Galveston was located on an uncertain boundary, and thus, was an ideal meeting place for freebooters to dispose of their contraband and take on fresh supplies."[46] Therefore, Galveston's geographic location was ideal for smuggling and other illegal trade, even in its earliest years. Interestingly, the Maceo family participated in the same behaviors one hundred years later.

Jean Lafitte occupied Galveston Island until 1820, when United States officials ordered him off the island. By that time, the majority of the Karankawas had been wiped out by the arrival of the Europeans. The Indians were described by early visitors as simple people, with few tools or weapons. Therefore, when the new settlers approached them violently, the natives were unable to protect themselves.[47] The newcomers viciously killed many. Those who survived the attacks were faced with another threat: disease. The group simply could not survive the spread of European diseases, as seen upon Cabeza de Vaca's arrival.

After Jean Lafitte's departure, the remaining Karankawas were killed or absorbed into other groups, thus disappearing from the scene. Many died when troops attacked them while the few survivors were distracted with performing a ritual dance.[48] After the island had been cleared of Lafitte and the Karankawas, plans were laid for Galveston to become a port for Mexico, which gained its independence from Spain in 1821. But settlements on the island were being reshaped by events leading up to Texas's Declaration of Independence in 1836. After the brief Texas Revolution, Galveston became a base for the Texas navy.[49]

Galveston Island was formally settled as a Mexican territory when Michel Menard made his payment for the eastern side of the island. This eastern portion, like the northern edge, was named after Bernardo de Gálvez, who had served as the viceroy of New Spain, or Mexico. Gálvez was responsible for the first cartographer hired to map the island. The cartographer named the land he mapped after his employer.[50] However, it was not until long after Galvez had died that Menard and Samuel May Williams officially obtained a charter for the city of Galveston in 1838, when the community lay within the Republic of Texas.[51] The name became commonly used for both the island and the city, as well as the bay that attracted so much traffic, both legal and illegal.

As can be seen in its earliest years, Galveston often became a residence for controversial groups. The Karankawas may have participated in cannibalism. Then, European explorers and settlers eradicated the natives. They, in turn, were replaced by one of the earliest organized crime groups: pirates. Even then, the port's location was exploited for illegitimate means. The geographic advantages of Galveston continued to provide a foundation for the local economy into the next century.

Upon being chartered as a city, Galveston quickly established its major trade routes and a culture of its own. The island soon became the largest exporter of cotton. Furthermore, it developed a nighttime livelihood that also became an economic force to be reckoned with. By the mid-1800s, there were a variety of saloons, as well as bordellos, or prostitution establishments.[52] The transient population, made up of sailors and immigrants, who frequented the establishments perpetuated these vice activities.

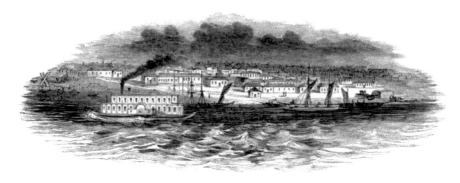

The Port of Galveston was depicted in the *Illustrated London News* in 1845, prior to many advancements but also prior to many catastrophes. *Courtesy of the Library of Congress.*

Throughout the years of the Civil War, Galveston was vulnerable to attacks. As a result, Fort Point was established on the island. Confederate troops were placed at this fort to protect Galveston from the invasion of Union soldiers. Before Union forces occupied the island city, all male Galvestonians were required to enlist in the army of the Confederacy. Furthermore, by 1862, the Confederates had complete control of the city, as well as the shipments coming in. This all came to an end when the Union army arrived in October 1862, but port activity resumed the following year when Confederate soldiers took back the island and its valuable port.[53]

Overall, the Civil War clearly had a significant impact on Galveston. Whether that impact was good or bad continues to be debated. Local historian Susan W. Hardwick argues that the war further handicapped Galveston's growth. She states that, in general, the war generated a great sense of insecurity among the residents on the island. Furthermore, the island suffered notable damage throughout the four years. Hardwick states, "Fences, homes, barns, and outbuildings had been ripped apart for firewood, army defensive mounds still ringed the town, and cannonballs were lodged in the walls of homes and buildings throughout the city."[54]

Other writers believe the Civil War had a positive influence on Galveston. Because of the island city's location and importance throughout these turbulent years, there was a strong economic interest in the port's accessibility. These discussions gained the attention of the Army Corps of Engineers. However, this group of engineers was not focused on Galveston solely for the benefit of that community. The corps of engineers was the result of President Thomas Jefferson's emphasis on national improvement.[55]

Galveston was one of the locations that benefited from this idea of national improvement. The corps came to the island after the Civil War with an elaborate plan to deepen the harbor. In conjunction with the growth of the American railroad system, the deepening of Galveston Harbor led to an increase in exports for the port city. This particular time represented the beginning of Galveston's most prosperous years. With the new system of railroads, Galveston enjoyed a greater connection to the burgeoning West. The western states found it was cheaper to send shipments to Galveston, rather than all the way across the country to the Atlantic ports.[56]

Perhaps both Hardwick and Young make valid points. The Civil War *did* have lasting effects on the island. However, the deepening of the harbor was not the only benefit experienced during this time. The underworld of Galveston felt the ripple effect of the presence of so many soldiers and sailors. The soldiers stationed at Fort Point and elsewhere in the area, as well as the sailors regularly coming in and out of the harbor, provided a new, and very large, customer base for the saloons and bordellos.[57]

As previously explained, these illicit institutions had been on the island for years. Yet these establishments experienced a tremendous growth throughout the Civil War era, which was especially due to the city's increased traffic. Throughout the war, civilian and military travelers regularly made trips into the port, and they often frequented the island city's many illicit institutions. This growth of Galveston's vice crime continued into the twentieth century. By 1927, a study regarding Galveston's red-light district found that "there were an estimated 1,000 ladies of the evening, 50 bordellos, and 13 other 'questionable houses.'"[58] Furthermore, the island community reportedly claimed "more saloons (489) than any city of comparable size and more than any other Gulf port—including New Orleans."[59]

The military men became regulars at the city's saloons and bordellos, despite Confederate army restrictions on alcohol and the illegality of prostitution. It is even reported that sailors received a discounted price when they came in—they received a five-dollar deal for thirty minutes rather than the regular price of ten dollars. In addition to the young men's presence in saloons and bordellos, they also spent money in the island's gambling establishments.[60] Of course, these behaviors did not stop when the Civil War ended in 1865, as evidenced by the continuing growth of Galveston's vice operations.

Immigrants provided another new customer base for these illegal businesses. Before and after the Civil War, Galveston experienced an influx of immigrants. At the time of the first postwar federal census in 1870, 40 percent of Galveston's population was made up of German immigrants. Overall, the island was the home of 13,818 residents that year. The impressive rate of immigration into Galveston continued until 1875, when federal laws limited the admission of new immigrants.[61] Nevertheless, immigrants continued to gain entry to Galveston.

As mentioned, there was already a large German population settled on the island prior to the Civil War. This particular group continued to represent the largest number of Galveston's foreign-born population at the turn of the century. As noted earlier, even today, a substantial German ancestry is found among Galvestonians. By 1900, the island's population had increased to a total of 37,788 residents, an increase since 1865 that closely matched the tripling of the Texas population during the same decades. Of those living in Galveston, 2,450 were German. There were also large Irish and Italian populations at the time of the 1900 census; 834 residents reported being born in Ireland, and 560 said they were from Italy. Overall, Galveston had a total of 7,328 emigrants from countries such as England, Scotland, France and Norway.[62] In short, almost 1 in 5 residents of Galveston in 1900 was born outside of the United States.

It is important to understand the effects such large number of immigrants would have had on the island. Overall, people from different cultural backgrounds tend to have varying ideas and moral beliefs regarding certain issues. Although some actions are considered *mala in se*, certain behaviors are not so widely denounced. Such behaviors are typically what make up an underworld. This was just as true for Galveston.

For example, among the Germans, Irish and Italians, Catholicism was often practiced. Catholicism teaches temperance. This meant the majority of Catholics believed that alcohol was acceptable, as long as it was consumed in moderation.[63] This had a huge effect on Galveston's social life throughout the Prohibition era. With such a large portion of the island population being immigrants, among whom drinking was accepted, saloon sales were strong, and they were enhanced by the frequent arrival of passenger ships. Furthermore, the island was never officially dry throughout Prohibition.

However, it is important to recall that these immigrant groups made up a mere fraction of the cultural diversity of Galveston. As discussed above, early European explorers and settlers, pirates and Civil War soldiers and sailors all came to Galveston. All of these groups brought different sets of ideals and values to the island. Therefore, just as the immigrants created a larger tolerance for alcohol on the island, the various transient groups of Galveston seemed to have created a tolerance for activities in general that fell into that same moral gray area.

Galveston provided an environment where conflicting ideas came together. In communities with a general consensus among residents or a primarily homogeneous population, these activities would not have survived as long as they did in Galveston. However, the diverse population provided diverse morals and practices. The resulting atmosphere set the stage for mobsters such as Sam and Rose Maceo. This meant that Galveston was open for business, even unlawful business.

Yet even for the law-abiding residents on the island, there were advantages to allowing these activities to continue. First, a significant portion of locals also enjoyed taking advantage of and participating in the businesses themselves. Secondly, because they benefited from the profitability of such businesses, legitimate or not, locals preferred to ignore the prevalence of vice in Galveston. This was especially true after the turn of the century, when Galveston lost its lead as the largest seaport in Texas. After a century of several setbacks, Galveston was desperate to find a new means of profitability.

THE TEMPESTUOUS TRIALS OF GALVESTON

During the nineteenth century, Galveston was faced with many obstacles. There was widespread disease, which diminished the island's population. There were numerous hurricanes. There was a horrible fire on the Strand, the main business district for the island city. As mentioned, the Civil War destroyed many of the island's structures. Galvestonians were constantly challenged throughout the 1800s. Although the island experienced significant growth throughout the century, it was also faced with many hindrances. It seemed that every time Galveston made progress, it was soon followed by retrogression.

The island was plagued with yellow fever outbreaks numerous times. Local historian Mary W. Remmers argues that the island suffered from only two separate epidemics, once in 1838 and again in 1867.[64] But historian David G. McComb cites twelve different occasions when Galvestonians suffered from yellow fever.[65] Some of these outbreaks of disease were clearly much worse than others. Reportedly, Galveston experienced a terrible storm and one of the earliest yellow fever outbreaks, just before the island city received its charter in 1838. Between these two events, Galveston lost more than 10 percent of its population. Then again in 1867, over 8,000 Galvestonians presented symptoms of yellow fever. In the end, 1,171 lives were lost to that particular epidemic.[66]

In addition to the substantial number of people who succumbed to yellow fever, Galveston also lost a significant portion of its population to hurricanes.

By the end of the century, Galveston had earned a deadly reputation. The island faced at least eleven hurricanes throughout the 1800s. However, these numbers are based partly on Indian legends and unofficial records. One estimate suggests even higher numbers—Hardwick argues that between 1810 and 1886, Galveston laid in the path of sixteen major storms.[67]

Although an official number of storms is hard to determine, it is clear the island suffered severe damage from multiple storms. As mentioned, Galveston was faced with a hurricane that almost ruined the island community's application for a charter. The storm hit in October 1837. According to locals' reports, only one person fell victim to the hurricane. However, after it had raged for three days and three nights, eight ships were left stranded on dry ground. Some residents considered the force of nature experienced in this storm to be an exception to the rest. For others, this hurricane was an indication of the dangers of the island, so they quickly relocated farther inland.[68]

For those who stayed, a new style of architecture was adopted in order to protect their belongings from the floodwaters of future storms. It was after this storm that the island's first customhouses were erected. These new structures were built on stilts to prevent future flooding and destruction. Plus the raised houses allowed more of the afternoon breeze from the ocean, an appealing quality in such a humid environment.[69] This style was the first of its kind and quickly became the style across the island. Presently, many houses continue to stand on and be built on stilts, just as they were two centuries ago.

In 1875, the Texas port city of Indianola suffered severe damages from a passing storm. Eleven years later, Indianola again suffered devastating losses in a hurricane. After the storm in 1886, Indianola citizens abandoned their homes for safer residences. Galvestonians witnessed the damage endured by their neighbors in Indianola. After seeing the city abandoned, Galvestonians began requesting protection for their own city. They demanded some assurance of safety from the inevitable future storms.[70]

The pattern of progression and retrogression continued into the twentieth century. After establishing itself as a city and overcoming many obstacles, Galveston faced near defeat in 1900. On the evening of September 8, what has become known as the Great Storm of 1900 devastated the island. The storm caused more deaths than any other natural disaster in American history. Estimates of the total death count vary between six thousand and twelve thousand. The actual number will never be known.[71]

The reports of destruction flooded out of Galveston in the days after the 1900 storm. The initial telegram reporting the damage stated:

Ruin is everywhere. Electric-light and telegraph poles are nearly all prostrated and the streets are littered with timbers, slate, glass, and every conceivable character of debris. There is hardly a habitable house in the city, and nearly every business house is badly damaged...From Tremont to P streets, thence to the beach, not a vestige of a residence is to be seen. In the business section of the city the water is from three to ten feet deep.[72]

Overall, the storm had nearly wiped Galveston off the map in the same fashion that the storm of 1886 had wiped their neighbor Indianola off the map. But Galveston would survive.

The Great Storm of 1900 did lead to significant change in Galveston. Many improvements occurred in response to the hurricane. For example, city officials began devising a plan to alleviate the harm caused by future storms. Prior to the devastation in 1900, Galveston residents were under the false impression that if a storm like the one that destroyed Indianola were to hit the island, Galveston Bay would absorb a large portion of the overall impact.[73] This had proven to be false, and as a result of the devastation, three engineers were selected to construct more proper precautions, such as a strong seawall and an elevation of many portions of the island city by pumping sand.

Rebuilding the city included replenishing its population. Prior to the Great Storm of 1900, Galveston had been a popular destination for many immigrants. In the later half of the nineteenth century, a cheap entertainment for Galvestonians was to go to the docks and witness the new influx of arrivals disembarking, often carrying or wearing clear evidence of their cultural heritages.[74] However, after the Great Storm of 1900, the city encouraged more new immigrants than ever before to settle on Galveston Island. The port community had already begun to experience a slowing of population growth prior to the destruction of the storm. Now it was germane to their survival to rebuild, not just the city, but also the city's population. Therefore, at the turn of the century, a new wave of immigrants was welcomed to Galveston, while locals focused on reconstructing a city.

Sam and Rose Maceo did not arrive on the island for ten more years, but even then, Galveston was still recovering from the Great Storm of 1900. While continuing to fall behind the lead of Houston, Galveston was looking for greater growth in its economy, as well as in its population. After the destruction of so many businesses in the storm, the two Maceo brothers eventually provided work to 10 percent of the island's population.[75]

Furthermore, their illicit activities made Galveston an appealing location after so much uncertainty left by the storm. This fact boosted the city's new investment in tourism.

A DEFINITIVE DECLINE

Despite the problems faced by islanders throughout the nineteenth century, Galveston developed into a flourishing city. It grew to be one of the richest cities in the United States, exceeded only by Providence, Rhode Island.[76] However, Galveston depended almost exclusively on its port activities. Unlike cities located farther inland, most of Galveston was not useful for farming. Floods and storms had distributed large amounts of salt across large portions of the island, making the land infertile. Therefore, other cities used Galveston as a port to ship their commodities in and out of the state. As a result, Galveston became one of the top exporters for cotton, shipping to New York, New Orleans and Great Britain.[77]

While the Northeast embraced the Second Industrial Revolution, Galveston did not. The island city never made the transition into a site for many of the newly introduced industries. Originally, local officials blamed the poor water supply. Despite these claims, by the 1890s, the island had a complete water system yet still failed to experience a rush of wealthy industrialists. A newcomer to Galveston, O.P. Hurford, explained to city officials that many outside companies were convinced that the island was unsafe. Because of the threat of floods and devastation from potential storms, they did not want to invest in the island, whose history clearly indicated that their concerns about hurricanes were not unfounded. Therefore, Galveston continued to serve as an importer and exporter for products made in other cities.[78]

While Galveston's growth slowed during the last quarter of the nineteenth century, Houston and other Texas cities flourished. In 1880, Galveston had the largest population of any community in the state, sitting at twenty-two thousand citizens. However, by 1890, Dallas and San Antonio had grown larger than the island city. By 1900, Houston had also bypassed Galveston. This shift in growth was the result of many contributing factors. As mentioned earlier, Galveston, unlike other cities, did not join the Second Industrial Revolution due to the physical nature of the island. Furthermore, Houston became one of the ports on the Gulf of Mexico that reaped the benefits of the oil explosion in Texas after Spindletop erupted in 1901. Again, Galveston did not grow with this new industry, either.[79]

Perhaps the island city's failure to invest in these new industries was due to its commitment of financial resources to other projects. Prior to the hurricane, Galveston had provided for growth by improving its port facilities. The depth of a harbor determined its class. A first-class harbor was required to "accommodate a ship drawing 26 feet of water at low tide." Originally, Galveston was considered a third-class harbor, and its depth increasingly became a problem. This status was due to two sandbars, with a shallow depth of eight to twelve feet, that encircled the island. With the Galveston Harbor Bill in 1890, the channels were deepened, and it was converted into a first-class harbor.[80] The island city thus recommitted itself to commerce, not industry.

Later, during the years after the Great Storm of 1900, while many other port cities were prospering from the Second Industrial Revolution and the new oil industry, Galveston leaders were working to increase its elevation and build a seawall. A group of leaders voted to raise the island's elevation to 18 feet, which would decline by 1 foot every 1,500 feet. In addition, a three-mile wall was constructed on the eastern edge of Galveston.[81] These drastic, and expensive, changes were seen as necessary steps to protect the island from another deadly storm.

It is likely that Galvestonians feared becoming like their old neighbors. As discussed, Indianola was essentially wiped off the Texas map in the 1886 hurricane. Afterward, the previous location of Indianola was no more than a sandy beach. For fear of becoming the memory of a city that was, Galvestonians stood strong and took the steps necessary to protect themselves from future storms. This prohibited the city from directing its resources toward the growth of new industries as discussed above. Furthermore, Houston became a more active port during this time, making it an even stronger opponent.

In 1866, the Houston Direct Navigation Company was established, which transferred cotton from the city to ships in Galveston Bay via river barges. By creating this company, Houstonians avoided using Galveston as their port city. Moreover, with technological advances, Houston leaders were able to increase the depth of Buffalo Bayou. Therefore, Houston became its own port—the city no longer had to use Galveston for the movement of many of its commodities. Houston had found a way to completely bypass Galveston for imports and exports. Furthermore, with the laying of railroads through North Texas, Galveston was not needed to transport commodities going to and from New Orleans. With these advances, Galveston lost more and more business.[82]

As Galveston thus went through changes after the Great Storm of 1900, nearby cities, especially ports, were also going through changes. Houston was flourishing in some of Galveston's darkest days. As noted earlier, by the beginning of the twentieth century, Houston's population had bypassed that of Galveston. By 1920, Houston's census reflected a population four times the size of Galveston's.[83] It was clear that Galveston's most prosperous days might be behind it. The residents of the island city understood that, to ensure the survival of their community, they needed to embrace the geographic resources that Galveston offered. Therefore, like many sandbar communities, Galveston largely became a tourist destination, despite the opposition of many locals.

The city's residents acknowledged the new source of revenue, even if some of them disliked it. Tourists had already started traveling to the beach for weekends and holidays throughout the year, but especially during the warmer seasons. The Galveston Surf Bathing Company was established in 1881. The company provided bathhouses along the majority of the coast.[84] The Galveston Pavilion was opened where the train tracks ended. Then, in 1883, the Beach Hotel was constructed. Unfortunately, the new hotel was not a profitable business and was suspiciously burned down shortly after the owner filed for insurance on the location. Also, the pavilion did not prosper long.[85] Nevertheless, other hotels on the island, such as the Tremont Hotel, continued to attract more tourists.

Aside from the hotels that were built along the beach, the city also offered other attractions. For example, the Grand Opera House was constructed in 1894.[86] The design and style of the new opera house reflected that of a great opera house in Europe. Furthermore, Galveston offered entertainment such as ballet and comedy clubs. The community earned a reputation for being ahead of its time. As Ace Collins wrote, "With forty miles of streetcar lines, 2,028 telephones, and two automobiles, Galveston was truly a modern city during a period when most of Texas was still largely a wide-open frontier."[87] Unfortunately for those who sought more substantial economic development, it became a city primarily focused on tourism after the Great Storm of 1900 undermined any other significant alternatives.

Sam and Rose Maceo contributed to the growth of Galveston within the established focus on tourism. In the 1920s, the brothers opened their first club, which attracted people from all over the country. From that point forward, Sam and Rose continued to open popular establishments. One location purchased by them was on the new seawall at Twenty-first Street. This particular spot went through numerous name changes, eventually becoming the famous, or maybe infamous, Balinese Room. The Balinese Room contributed largely toward the growth in Galveston's tourism. With nationally recognized entertainers, gambling, alcohol and fine dining, tourists came from far and wide to experience the Balinese Room.

Despite the modern improvements on the island, it is clear that Galveston was faced with many obstacles throughout its early history. The city was devastated over and over by epidemics and hurricanes, particularly the Great Storm of 1900, during its first century of development. Large businesses would not come to the island out of fear of destruction by future natural disasters. Economically, the island city was later bypassed by other Texas cities and ports. All in all, these circumstances likely influenced the tolerance of the residents when the Maceos arrived in the early 1900s. For the Maceos brought with them profit and growth, something the Galvestonians were hungry for after such setbacks.

As previously explained, Galveston was built around a transient population. This population was extremely diverse, with a high proportion of immigrants with various cultural and religious backgrounds. Having such a heterogeneous populace, the island had adopted a more relaxed and open way of life. With such cultural multiplicity, there was an overall emphasis on free will. However, this island-wide attitude was not the only explanation for the success of vice. As described, the island was desperate for new growth and economic stimulation. That is what the underworld provided, and these illegitimate businesses promoted the growth of legitimate enterprises.

Prior to the arrival of the Maceo family, Galveston had already developed an underworld. The island city was home to two organized crime groups. Although already in existence, these gangs did not gain significant power on the island until Prohibition began. With the exclusion of alcohol, the two organizations enjoyed a new and very large market for smuggling illegal liquor into Galveston through its port. With such a high demand, this quickly became a lucrative business. The Maceos understood this situation and infiltrated the businesses. This was the beginning of their rise to the top of Galveston's underworld and the beginning of their empire.

3

CREATING PERFECT MOBSTERS

CULTURAL AND SOCIAL INFLUENCES

E ven before Sam and Rose Maceo arrived in Galveston, organized crime was not a foreign idea to the brothers. Their family came to the United States from a region where organized crime had occurred for years. As historian Stephen L. Mallory has carefully explained, all mafia and organized crime activity conducted by Italians in the United States can be traced back to the island of Sicily.[88] Although there are no indications that the two brothers were involved in Sicilian mafia activity, it is reasonable to assume that they retained some of their Italian heritage when they traveled across the Atlantic Ocean. This would have included an understanding of mafia activities. Moreover, it is likely the two young brothers would have shared in the popular Sicilian support for the mafia.

Just as Galveston had a history of vice crime, so did Sicily, and in part, the two histories are linked. The Maceo family's native land was known for such activities. Also similar to Galveston, the organized crime of Sicily was the result of a long, turbulent history. In both areas, social and economic circumstances began to decline during the nineteenth century. The sad events that occurred throughout that century in both locations led to the rise of criminal activity and support for criminal groups from many average citizens.

Sam and Rose came to America with their family in search of greater opportunity. Immigrating to the United States was an attempt to escape the unfavorable conditions that had plagued Sicily for decades. As stated, the brothers likely had a basic understanding of organized crime when they arrived in America. Upon settling in their new location, the brothers encountered groups of Sicilians who had organized and were participating in mafia activities similar to those they had observed (or perhaps participated in) on their native island. The Maceos also realized that their economic conditions had not significantly improved when they crossed the ocean, contrary to what they had expected. Plus they understood that the illicit activities of the criminal groups provided a quick profit. Therefore, it was not long before these cultural factors drew the brothers into organized crime along the Gulf Coast, specifically in Galveston.

CULTURAL CATALYSTS FOR A CAREER IN CRIME

Throughout the 1800s, Italy went through many transformations. In 1797, the French invaded the Italian peninsula. After a couple of defeats, they achieved and maintained control from 1808 until 1814.[89] However, in 1815, Austria regained control of the area. Despite the subsequent return to a decentralized state system, the liberal ideals of the French, especially the notion of national unity, left a lasting impression on Italians. After years of unrest under the restored system and many failed revolutions, a war to unify Italy once again erupted in 1859.[90] The following year, Giuseppe Garibaldi and his "famous Redshirts" liberated Sicily from its Bourbon rulers.[91]

Despite the successful unification of Italy, Sicilians were still suffering from an economic depression when the century came to an end. Sicily's most lucrative markets were suffering under new taxations. Furthermore, the many peasants who lived in the region believed they were particularly being targeted by new policies and programs, which tended to favor the upper and middle classes yet perpetuated their own poor conditions.[92] Under these pressures, frustrations grew, as did a lack of trust in the government. Ultimately, this led to an increase in organized criminal activity, or the mafia.

Additionally, the new government was unable, or possibly unwilling, to offer aid to the southern Italians, who were frequently treated like an inferior group. Sicilians were often referred to as "Africans" and treated like criminals by the new national government.[93] This unstable environment provided even more opportunity for the previously established organized crime groups. Peasants and small landowners looked to these organizations to fill the absence of local law enforcement. As island conditions became progressively less favorable, the mafia received more and more support from locals. Even the Catholic church gave support to these criminal groups because of the protection and aid they provided to the community.[94]

In an effort to rid Sicily of violent criminals, the new government invaded the citizens' privacy and homes and killed innocent people in an attempt to capture or kill the not so innocent.[95] In response to the official violence, as well as the ongoing economic depression, Sicilians began emigrating in mass numbers. One study claims that "an average of 117,596 persons left Italy annually during the decade 1871–80."[96]

The Maceo family, like thousands before them, also sought refuge in a new country. They hoped to find better economic conditions and a higher standard of life when they arrived in the United States. They also hoped to find relief from the oppression that had been endured for so many years in Sicily. Louisiana had already established itself as a popular destination for Italian immigrants. Therefore, the Maceos embarked for the largest city of the American South: New Orleans.[97]

Although Sam and Rose Maceo admittedly spent a limited time in their native country, each adopted certain qualities from Sicily before departing for the United States. According to Rose's census records and passenger list records, he resided in Sicily for only the first fifteen years of his life. Sam's records indicate that he may have stayed in southern Italy five more years than his younger brother.[98] Despite how briefly each brother resided in Sicily, they each carried with them traits from the Sicilian lifestyle and culture that would influence their decisions when they arrived in Galveston.

As mentioned, the various organized crime groups of Sicily, or mafia, received widespread support throughout the nineteenth century—even leaders of the Catholic Church were aware of the groups' activities and endorsed them. This was because the Sicilians had endured years of war, economic decline and lack of support and protection from the government. As a result, they accepted the local crime groups. They understood what the criminals were involved in but also realized that the criminals provided economic stimulation and safety to the communities.[99]

It is very likely that the Maceos in Sicily shared this support for mafia groups. Their family, too, would have experienced the impact of the devastating social conditions. They left their country for the same reasons thousands of other immigrants did—for new opportunities in the United States. Thus, they would have well understood both the positive and negative consequences of having crime groups. Furthermore, the Maceos would have observed how these groups involved themselves in the community and gained the trust of locals.

When the Maceos arrived in New Orleans, they encountered an entirely new world, which was also in turmoil. Officials in Louisiana were interested in increasing the number of incoming European immigrants. After the Civil War ended, these officials recognized the need for more laborers, specifically for rural laborers. Thus, there began an immigration movement in which appointed local representatives essentially advertised for the labor of immigrants.[100]

Conveniently, it was largely rural workers who were leaving Sicily during this time. Rural workers particularly had begun to suffer under the economic depression in Italy. Although many Louisianans saw the potential of these immigrants, there were a large number of locals who had reservations about the matter. For example, neither farmers nor former slaves wanted lots of immigrants infiltrating the southern job market.[101] In addition to the local residents opposing the immigrants for economic reasons, Louisianans were particularly opposed to immigration from Sicily. They believed that the Sicilians were an inferior race.

Overall, this resistance undermined the campaign to lure many immigrants to Louisiana. Furthermore, Sicilian immigrants knew they would receive more support and acceptance in the Northeast, where large Italian populations had already settled. Although the Louisiana campaign was not as successful as its officials had hoped it would be, there were still many immigrants who entered the southern state throughout this period.

Although Sicilian immigrants were aware of the disdain that many Louisianans held for their race, the southern port of New Orleans did have certain appealing characteristics. According to historian Thomas Reppetto, many Sicilians preferred New Orleans to northeastern ports. New York and ports in the New England states, such as Boston, did not much resemble their homeland. New Orleans, on the other hand, had rich Spanish and French influences, much like their tiny island. The city celebrated with many festivals (especially Catholic ones), had a well-known tendency to be inattentive toward vice activities and even had the same diseases as those suffered in Sicily.[102]

People also claimed that the weather in New Orleans was similar to that in Sicily. Historian Jean M. Brown stated that many Sicilians preferred New Orleans due to the port's familiar climate, which was good for producing many of the same crops found back home.[103] New Orleans was warm and humid, much like their island across the Atlantic. On the other hand, the Northeast suffered from erratic and unpredictable weather, not to mention cold winter storms, to which the Sicilians were not accustomed. Apparently, recruiters failed to mention the erratic hurricanes that hit the southern coast, including the storm that devastated Galveston in 1900.

During the late nineteenth century, more than 130,000 Italians emigrated from their country to the United States. For the American South, there was a push from the oppression experienced in Sicily and a pull from local efforts to recruit immigrants. Because of the appealing features of New Orleans, the southern port experienced a dramatic increase in immigration, including Italians. Pre–Civil War estimates of the Italian population ranged around several thousand. However, by 1890, that number had increased to approximately 25,000, a significant proportion of whom were from Sicily.[104] So, despite the fact that the newcomers continued to suffer persecution and harassment similar to that which had been plaguing Sicily for years, Sicilians entered the South, and New Orleans, at massive rates.

Major cities that received high numbers of immigrants, such as New York, frequently experienced high rates of unemployment and overcrowding. Furthermore, these cities typically became associated with some degree of organized crime. But new arrivals in the Northeast were not the only immigrants who became involved in organized crime.[105] These problems also became prevalent in New Orleans, where many immigrants, including Italians, were recruited for field labor and then later went astray.

Partly as a result of the Louisiana immigration movement, there were a growing number of immigrants to that state. As pointed out, the lifestyle and climate there appealed to many Italians, especially Sicilians. Thus, Italians reportedly made up the largest immigrant group in New Orleans.[106] And just as Italians in New York experienced a disturbing correlation between growing populations and deteriorating social conditions, those in New Orleans also experienced negative changes within their community.

When many European immigrants arrived in the United States, they found that conditions had not really improved for them after moving across the Atlantic Ocean. The oppression and poor quality of life that many of them were attempting to escape were still issues when they settled in America. As a result, groups responded in much the same way they did in their native countries. Just as Italians had responded to a low quality of life in Sicily with brigandage and organized crime, so did the Italians who had resettled in New Orleans and the surrounding cities.[107]

This was often the result of a false hope for better opportunities. Rather than working as free laborers, many newly arrived Italians fell victim to peonage.[108] Many immigrant laborers were basically relegated to roles similar to that of the South's former slaves, recently freed under the Thirteenth

Amendment but most often economically confined to farms as sharecroppers and tenants. The oppression felt by the newly arriving residents also led to voluntary and involuntary social segregation. The locals frequently shunned them, but they also naturally banded together for support.

These minority communities quickly fostered the environment for illegal activities similar to those found in their native country. In Sicily, groups had gathered and called themselves "La Cosa Nostra" in response to the harsh social and economic conditions the Sicilians faced.[109] As Mallory explained, "To survive, the unemployed began to commit criminal acts and then form gangs for power and profits."[110] When the Italians arriving in the United States suffered from the same social circumstances, they again resorted to organized crime, and their operations were often referred to as mafia activities.

The Maceo family was one of the thousands of families that relocated from Sicily to the United States during this turbulent time. However, this particular family's arrival would have a lasting effect on the Gulf Coast that no one could have anticipated. They spent a brief time among the thousands of other Italian immigrants in Louisiana before relocating. Nevertheless, this brief time was long enough for one of the brothers to gain an insider's perspective on organized crime in America.

THE MACEOS SETTLE IN AMERICA

When the Maceos arrived in the United States, they discovered, like many other immigrants, that things were not much different from back home. In Louisiana, the Sicilians were not favored, so groups of Italians formed small communities. These communities suffered from continued poverty, which resulted in the same organized crime that had occurred on their native island. It comes as no surprise, then, that one of the brothers quickly became involved in his first organized crime group. Through such an organization, Sam learned a few quick lessons in the mafia trade. When the brothers moved to Galveston, they were equipped with the necessary tools to participate in the island city's criminal activity.

Rosario "Rose" Maceo was born in Palermo, on the island of Sicily in Italy, on June 8, 1887. He departed from his native country as a young teenager, sailing across the Atlantic Ocean and arriving in Louisiana in 1901.[111] Yet the rest of his family initially remained in Palermo. His parents,

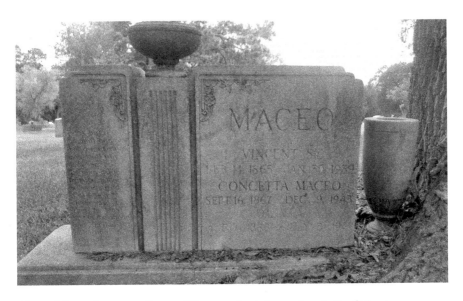

Vincent Maceo, brother to Sam and Rose, was buried near them in the Galveston Memorial Park Cemetery, alongside his wife. *Courtesy of Amanda Belshaw.*

Vittorio, or "Vito," and Angelina, as well as his siblings, Olivia, Salvatore or "Sam," Frank and Vincenzo or "Vincent," joined him in the United States throughout the following decade. Olivia was the eldest of the five Maceo children who came to the United States. Vincent, who was a mere six years old when he arrived with his parents in 1902, was the youngest. The Maceo family, including Rose, first settled in Leesville, an agricultural community in Louisiana.[112]

In age, and perhaps in other aspects, Sam was Rose's closest brother. He was born on November 24, 1890. Sam sailed to America aboard the *Liguria*, departing from Palermo on September 18, 1910. It took two weeks to cross the Atlantic and land at the port of New Orleans.[113] At the time of his arrival, Sam was almost twenty years old. He had a mere thirteen dollars in his pocket when he stepped off the ship. As expected, he joined his family who had already arrived in the United States and initially settled in Leesville.

The Maceo family's time in Louisiana was very limited. Nevertheless, this is where Sam was given his first opportunity to apply the knowledge he brought from Sicily. It was in an Italian neighborhood of New Orleans called Little Palermo where he first became involved in the activities of an organized crime syndicate. While living in Sicily, the brothers simply observed crime families as outsiders. Upon settling in New Orleans, Sam followed in his father's and brother's footsteps. He attended barber school to try to establish a career. Unfortunately, he continued to struggle financially as a barber and, shortly after, became involved with the local mafia.[114] Sam's involvement in the group, in the Sicilian-dominated streets of Little Palermo, provided him with new insider information.

Although some immigrants enjoyed success and fortune in the United States, most of them crowded into a single geographical region, which created poor social circumstances for the majority. For example, Little Palermo was described as "a crowded slum next to the waterfront."[115] As mentioned, densely populated urban areas tended to breed crime—specifically organized crime. Little Palermo was no exception. Still, Sam's brief involvement with the crime groups in that New Orleans neighborhood provided him with the chance to experience the hierarchy and politics of organized crime—something he mastered in his later years. Little Palermo prepared Sam to help Rose with the activities they would soon become involved with in Galveston.

Rose also continued to struggle financially. Working as a barber in Leesville did not provide a substantial income. Tired of the struggle in Louisiana, Rose left to settle in Galveston by 1912. There, he found greater financial success. Although the exact date is unclear, Sam joined his brother in Galveston a few years later. By 1917, Sam had claimed Galveston as his permanent address on a registration card for the World War I draft.[116]After Olivia followed her brothers to Galveston, she married Joseph Frances "Frank" Fertitta.[117] The marriage between Olivia and Frank created what would later prove to be a significant alliance for the Maceo family.

Mallory has described the circumstances under which organized crime typically develops. They include "severe overcrowding, rampant crime, disproportionate wealth, gang activity, corruption of public officials, widespread gambling, and prostitution."[118] When looking at Galveston, the island city already suffered from several of these characteristics. As explained in the previous chapter, there was already widespread gambling and prostitution on the island. There was corruption of public officials as explained by local historian Mary W. Remmers.[119] There was a lack of economic opportunity for many residents. And there was also gang activity already on the island.

The two gangs that were already present when Sam and Rose Maceo arrived were the Beach Gang and the Downtown Gang. O.E. "Dutch" Voight, a German immigrant, and his partner, Ollie J. Quinn, headed the Beach Gang. Although Voight had the final say in the gang's activities, Quinn was the recognized leader of the group. Voight was the first rumrunner in

Galveston. On the contrary, Johnny "Jack" Nounes and his partner, George Musey, led the Downtown Gang.[120]

Although the Beach Gang and Downtown Gang existed before Prohibition, when the Volstead Act was passed in 1919, the gangs' activities blossomed. Prior to the passing of the Volstead Act, Galveston had high rates of prostitution and gambling. Now the demand for alcohol had to be met through illegal channels, which provided a new trade for the criminal groups. At this point, the underworld in Galveston became intertwined in illicit partnerships outside the realms of the island; the gangs were receiving shipments of alcohol from various countries. The Beach Gang and Downtown Gang ultimately dominated the bootlegging business of Galveston. This period marked a growth in organized crime for the island city.

As the profits from illegal liquor imports rapidly increased, the gangs began to establish their territories. This marking of boundaries can be seen as the beginning of the two groups' fall. With new territories, there was more conflict between the Beach Gang and Downtown Gang. This was an important factor in the success of Sam and Rose Maceo. Although Galveston's history gave rise to a fertile environment for organized crime and the brothers' cultural experiences prepared them for a career in crime, the instability among the island's gangs provided the Maceos with an open pathway to the top of Galveston's underworld.

In order to understand how the Maceo brothers progressed so quickly, it is important to evaluate the gangs that existed when the brothers arrived in Galveston. Each of the two gangs suffered internal weaknesses. As frequently occurs, there were untrustworthy members in each group. Furthermore, the intergang competition had a remarkable impact on the brothers' progression. The gangs were killing each other, which inherently diminished the number of rungs the Maceos had to climb to get to the top of the ladder.

FROM ONE PORT CITY TO ANOTHER

By the time the Maceo family arrived in Galveston, island residents had experienced rapid and drastic changes. The city had suffered many setbacks, which eventually led to Houston's ascendancy in the transport business. Throughout the following decades, Houston continued to grow. Local writer Paul Burka claims that, at the beginning of the 1920s, Galveston Island was home to about eighty steamship companies. However, each of these companies slowly relocated to Houston.[121] Inevitably, the locals were forced to expand their possible tourist attractions. As the Maceos became Galvestonians, they aided in this development, creating a nationally recognized reputation.

Once again, organized crime was used to overcome the harsh reality of poverty. As mentioned, Galveston already harbored many characteristics known to produce crime. Not only did it appear to be the perfect location for a criminal organization, but the island had been built on a spirit of free will. Galveston Island had been the location of many illegitimate businesses, as well as many activities that were not widely accepted elsewhere. The Maceo brothers quickly found themselves in the middle of such illicit operations, many of which had clear links to tourism. They found this provided a quicker dollar than a career in barbering, just as the criminal activity in the Little Palermo neighborhood of New Orleans had also yielded a larger return.

Although the Maceo brothers, within a few years, were doing better in Galveston than they had been previously doing in Leesville, their particular trade did not render very profitable returns. The brothers were charging a

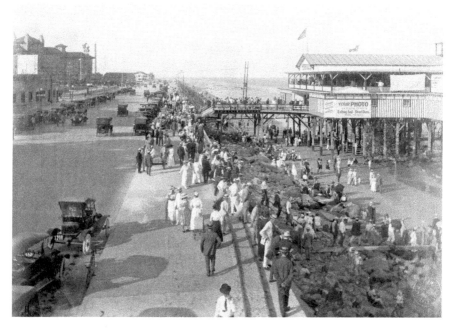

The first Murdoch's Bathhouse was constructed in the late 1800s. It was destroyed by the Great Storm, as well as various subsequent hurricanes, and was rebuilt each time. *Courtesy of the Rosenberg Library.*

mere twenty-five cents per haircut. When Sam joined his older brother in Galveston, Rose was working in a shop on Murdoch's Pier. Sam found work in the Galvez Hotel shortly after relocating. According to award-winning Texas journalist Gary Cartwright, it was Rose's work on the pier that first brought the brothers in contact with Galveston's vice crime and thus with a way to better their economic circumstances.[122]

Murdoch's Pier, where Rose cut hair, was a frequent hangout for Galveston's Beach Gang. As mentioned, Dutch Voight and Ollie Quinn led the Beach Gang. While working on the pier, Voight became a regular customer of Rose Maceo. Over time, Rose gained his client's trust. When the time came when Voight needed a favor, he knew who to ask.

In 1921, Voight received a large shipment that included 1,500 bottles of liquor.[123] Unfortunately for the Beach Gang, the shipment had been brought to the attention of a group of agents for the federal Bureau of Customs. The federal agents were working diligently to track it down. Voight was already on their radar, so he understood that his only option was to move

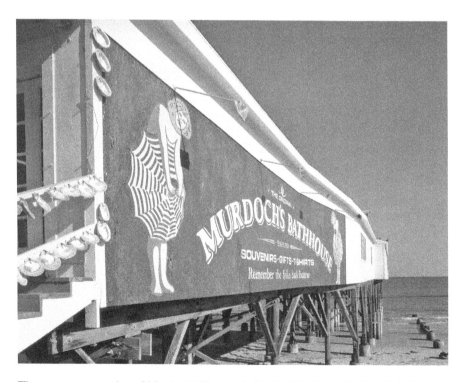

The most recent version of Murdoch's Pier was built after Hurricane Ike demolished the infamous location in 2008. *Courtesy of the Library of Congress.*

the shipment to a location that could not be traced back to him. Voight thus reached out to his barber, Rose Maceo.

Voight had previously been made aware of Rose's place of residency. Therefore, he knew that Rose had a space beneath his house, which was out of public view as a result of the increased elevation of Galveston in the years following the Great Storm of 1900. He asked Rose to store the bottles under his home for no more than three days, after which time the shipment would be divided and shipped elsewhere. Voight also informed Rose that he would be generously compensated $1 for each bottle stored under his home—a total of $1,500.[124]

Rose agreed, somewhat reluctantly. He and his brother Sam had participated in bootlegging as well, but on a much smaller scale.[125] During the holidays, the two had handed out bottles of bootlegged wine to some of their best clients. They inconspicuously passed the bottles in hollow loaves of bread. After the holidays had passed, Sam and Rose received many requests for more of their wine. Happy to oblige, and to make a profit, they continued to pass the bootlegged alcohol. When asked of his involvement in bootlegging years later, Sam reportedly told friends that the reason for selling his first bottle of bootlegged alcohol was to help pay for his mother's medical bills.[126]

Unlike these previous minor involvements, the request from Voight had much higher risks. The three nights that Rose slept over the 1,500 bottles were reportedly restless. However, when Voight came to retrieve the bootlegged liquor, Rose declined the agreed-upon payment. Instead, he asked for the money to be invested in future ventures and for him and his brother Sam to be involved in the Beach Gang's next deal. Voight and Quinn, knowing the Maceo brothers were trustworthy individuals, agreed to allow the two young men to participate in their operations. This marked the beginning of the Maceos' involvement in Galveston's organized crime.[127]

From this first venture forward, the Maceo brothers did not waste any time. It is reported that the same year the Maceo brothers became associated with the Beach Gang, Sam opened a soda stand, which served as a front business for bootlegging activities.[128] This was just the beginning of the construction of an empire. Soon, the Maceos were providing gambling opportunities for Galvestonians and tourists. They provided liquors and wines for the guests of their clubs, never letting Prohibition slow them down. Furthermore, they provided first-class entertainment that had never been brought to the South. These activities were uniquely placed under one roof—a popular idea that seemed to be instantly profitable.

Although Sam was a likeable character, as will be explained in subsequent chapters, it took more than a great personality to build a great empire. Each of the factors discussed thus far contributed to the brothers' success. Historical elements truly created a community that was open to illicit activities. Galveston thrived on entertainment and drinking. However, without the brothers' cultural background and previous understanding of organized crime in Sicily and then New Orleans, it is likely they would have faltered, much like the previous gangs on the island.

Nevertheless, Sam worked with poise to attract much positive attention to the Maceo family's businesses. As will be explained, he really did care for the island like a true Galvestonian. His brother Rose, although not as amiable, was still seen as a key player in the businesses. His role on the island was much different. Just as the brothers could not have succeeded without the trials and events that led to Galveston's free will attitude, they could not have succeeded without each other. Each Maceo brother played an essential role, which aided in the construction of an island empire that attracted nationwide attention.[129]

4

BUILDING AN EMPIRE

BOOTLEGGING, GAMBLING AND PROSTITUTION

From the 1920s to the 1950s, Galveston became known as the Free State of Galveston, an "open city" where Sam and Rose Maceo reigned.[130] But it was not the only city in Texas that offered gambling. Operators in Beaumont, Victoria, Corpus Christi, Fort Worth and Port Arthur also dabbled in the gambling business. As journalist Paul Burka has explained, the difference between Galveston and other Texas cities, such as those listed, was the fact that Galveston offered such activities everywhere. The Maceos were not the only operators of illicit businesses in Galveston, but they had the support of many of the locals and practiced their trade in the open. As a result, when a traveler left Harris County and entered Galveston County, he crossed the "Maceo-Dickinson line," a sardonic reference to the Maceos' control not only of vice operations in the city of Galveston but also in surrounding communities such as Dickinson.[131]

As explained, Sam and Rose Maceo became involved in Galveston's criminal activity when they were approached by Dutch Voight. Shortly after their initial business agreement, the two brothers became active members in the Beach Gang's activities. Throughout the next few years, they took advantage of the group's weaknesses. They used their knowledge regarding organized crime to advance in the organization. With their experiences, Sam and Rose were able to quickly progress to the top. Upon obtaining leadership of not just the Beach Gang but also the remaining members of their rival Downtown Gang the brothers began to build a legacy on the island.

When the Maceo brothers became involved in the Beach Gang's activities, the United States was at the height of Prohibition. Although the island's two gangs controlled the majority of the area's illicit activities, Galveston, as a popular port used for smuggling bootlegged liquors, attracted other rumrunners as well. Newspapers constantly ran articles regarding the port's illicit activities. They frequently reported stories such as "Rum Runners Captured off Galveston Coast."[132] Plus there were regular reports of suspicious ships being detained off the coast of Galveston.[133] The island's gangs obviously received much negative attention through many of the local news stories.

A major portion of the negative attention focused on these groups was due to the ongoing struggles between opposing members. As mentioned, Prohibition marked a new era for Galveston's vice crime. Due to the demand for liquor trafficking, there was more business coming into and going out of the island city. As a result of greater competition, there were also ongoing turf wars. Galveston became an area with frequent gun battles in the public streets and alleyways.[134]

There were several gang-related murders throughout the 1920s and 1930s. George Musey of the Downtown Gang was involved in a murder in which the victim was buried "head first in quick lime."[135] There is also a local legend that Rose Maceo killed his first wife. As journalist Robert Nieman claims, after Rose discovered that his wife was having an affair, both her body and that of her lover were found floating in Galveston Bay.[136] Locals seemed to enjoy this legend and continued to retell it. Perhaps it added to the dangerous character that had evolved around Rose.

However, the truth of the matter is it was not Rose's wife who was found dead. Rose actually has only one recorded marriage, to Frances Dispensa, and she outlived him by thirty years. Madge Maceo, early wife to Vincent Maceo, Rose's brother, was the woman found dead. There was no lover in the next grave; she was found alone in a group of bushes just off the road. Vincent, who found the body, was briefly held for questioning. He stated that his wife had been wearing expensive jewelry, which appeared to be missing when the body was discovered.[137] Despite the initial suspicion of Vincent, he was never charged for his wife's murder.

In the early 1930s, Rose *was* actually involved in one particular murder case. In April 1933, he was arrested in connection with and charged for the death of a local licensed pilot, Lee Hausinger, after the victim was found on a sidewalk shot twice.[138] However, Hausinger was not an innocent victim in the wrong place at the wrong time. Galveston police found that he was

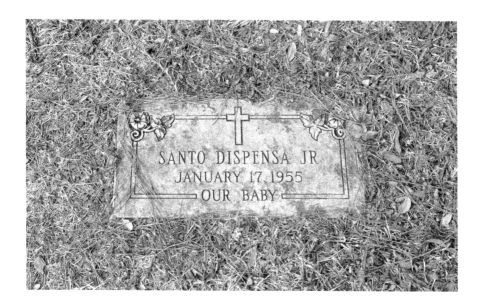

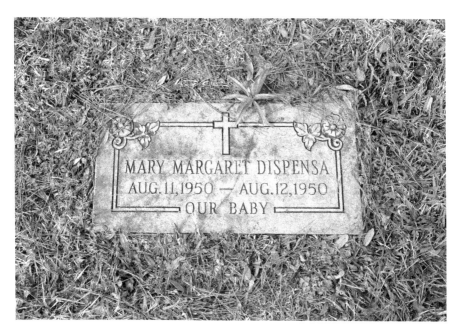

This page: Frances Dispensa married Rosario in 1922. After passing away, she was entombed with Rosario in his mausoleum. Directly outside are the headstones of two young Dispensas. *Courtesy of Amanda Belshaw.*

wanted in connection to the robbery of Joseph Frances "Frank" Fertitta, Olivia Maceo's husband, just hours before the shooting.[139] Plus he was being tried in another case of armed robbery and kidnapping.[140]

Soon after the shooting of Hausinger occurred, Rose Maceo surrendered to the police.[141] In the criminal case that ensued, a "Mrs. Bolton" testified that Hausinger told her that Rose had shot him. She stated that the dying victim said, "Listen, Cora and everybody, I want you all to know that Rose Maceo did it. He shot me in the back."[142] Despite such compelling evidence, the grand jury returned to no bill the murder case.[143] Rose received hardly more than a slap on the wrist.

These two cases just added to the mystery of Rose Maceo. As he and Sam moved to the top of Galveston's world of vice, Rose became known as the "enforcer" (for those who preferred to rely on traditional mafia terms).[144] Therefore, these cases helped develop the necessary character profile for Rose. Events such as these ensured Rose would be quite capable of effectively fulfilling his role in his brother's operations and his own.

Although the murders discussed depict a growing aggression on the island, these particular victims were members of neither the Beach Gang nor the Downtown Gang. Violence between the gang members themselves became a particular problem. Such violence was the product of a relentless battle for control over the island. There was a constant struggle within groups, as well as between groups. Therefore, as Sam and Rose Maceo climbed to the top of Galveston's underworld, they became intertwined with the dangerous encounters between the island's gangs.

Although vice has always been present in Galveston, there was a fierce competition for the businesses when the port became an open door for smuggled alcohol. Because of Galveston's geographical potential, interest was even received from individuals who were not local to the island. In particular, Al Capone became interested in the island's activities.

It is important to look back, before Prohibition, to understand why Capone had an interest in Galveston. Prior to this era, Johnny "Jack" Nounes of the Downtown Gang had a partner by the name of Francesco Raffaele "Frank" Nitti. Nitti was an Italian immigrant who had traveled to Galveston like many of the island's gang members. More specifically, Nitti was of Sicilian descent. However, Nitti did not stay in Galveston long. After briefly working with Nounes, he fled from Galveston with a stash of Nounes's cash and headed north to Chicago, with profits equaling $24,000.[145]

Upon reaching Chicago, Nitti partnered with Capone. According to Jean M. Brown's published master's thesis, Nitti possessed the Sicilian heritage that Capone was missing. Because Capone was not of Sicilian descent, he was unable to fully penetrate the organized crime of Chicago. However, by partnering with a Sicilian, in this case Nitti, Capone was finally able to form direct associations with other groups in the city. He was finally in the middle of Chicago's world of organized crime.[146]

After settling with Capone in Chicago, the man who had previously absconded from Galveston carrying Nounes's money became known as Frank "the Enforcer" Nitti. Working as Capone's right-hand man, Nitti became infamous for his work in Chicago.[147] However, while working alongside Capone, Nitti frequently told stories of the successful gangs on a tiny island off the coast of Texas. He explained that he had abandoned his involvement in the island's activities before Galveston experienced the full benefits of Prohibition. He told Capone of a burgeoning underworld in which they should become involved, by force if necessary.[148]

This is exactly what was attempted. Naturally, Capone became interested in Galveston and desired a part in its illegitimate profits. Therefore, he sent Nitti back to the island in order to make an offer to the Maceos. However, the Maceos and their associates were not eager to make a deal. There are varying versions regarding what happened when Nitti returned to the island city. Nevertheless, the consensus is that Nitti was either chased out of Galveston or removed from town and ordered never to return. Before Nitti departed from the island for his second time, Nounes required him to hand over the money he had previously stolen.[149] Following this encounter, there are no additional reports of Nitti ever returning to Galveston again.

This story illustrates the allure Galveston had, even before the Maceos arrived. The island city's activities attracted the attention of the infamous Capone. This also emphasizes the importance of the Maceo brothers' later success. Capone, who inflicted terror on Chicago throughout the early 1920s, did not have the power to penetrate Galveston's underworld. At the same time, as will be illustrated, even some gangs that had previously established themselves on the island were not strong enough to survive. The growth of the Maceo empire depended on the two brothers' personal abilities, as well as the previously discussed social and cultural aspects of Galveston that made it an open city.

At this point, it is necessary to look at the inter- and intragang dynamics in Galveston during Prohibition. The Downtown Gang and the Beach Gang fought to maintain their previously established territories. This meant conflict regularly occurred between the two groups. However, the gangs also faced constant internal struggles. Both types of struggles added to the violent gang warfare that was birthed under the Volstead Act.

Musey, leader of the Downtown Gang, caused the earliest conflict experienced by Sam and Rose Maceo and the rest of the Beach Gang. The Maceos, under Dutch Voight's oversight, had business in the North and Northwest, shipping alcohol as far as Cleveland. Their organization regularly received shipments of liquor through the port of Galveston before shipping them north. They also shipped alcohol to New Orleans. However, Musey managed to learn the route that was used between Galveston and New Orleans.[150]

As Galveston made more profits from Prohibition, the rivalry between the island's two gangs intensified. Musey began intercepting the Maceos' alcohol shipments between Galveston and New Orleans. He would openly buy and sell the shipments he confiscated from the Maceos' transport route to the "Big Easy."[151] When Sam and Rose learned what Musey was doing, they were outraged.

Nevertheless, the Maceo brothers apparently continued to bide their time. With Quinn still the leader of the Beach Gang and Voight still second in command, Sam and Rose were careful not to step on any toes. So even though the brothers were not at all happy about Musey's interceptions and his making a profit from them, they understood that they were in no position to retaliate.[152] With time, the brothers would finally return the favor to Musey. However, such an act would also involve the help of a disgruntled Downtown Gang member.

As previously mentioned, Musey was one of the leaders of the Downtown Gang who partnered with Nounes. In 1924, Nounes was jointly convicted with a man by the name of Joe Varnell.[153] It was discovered that the two were deeply involved in a conspiracy to "import, receive, transport and facilitate the transportation after importation of intoxicating liquor."[154] According to a newspaper article, their British schooner was carrying over 4,200 bottles of various liquors when it was intercepted.

About a year after the initial sentence, Nounes learned that his appeal had been denied and that he would indeed be required to serve two years in a federal prison and pay a fine of $5,000.[155] However, it did not take him long to reclaim his territory in Galveston. After being released, Nounes was again under suspicion in 1927. The second case concerned the activities at a club he managed. Texas attorney general Claude Pollard obtained an injunction to stop its operations after a search warrant yielded over $10,000 of gambling paraphernalia in the Roseland Dinner Club.[156]

In 1929, Nounes received his second liquor-related conviction. Nounes and Musey were both arrested months after the federal seizure of two ships bearing illegal liquors—the *Imperator* and the *Lena*, both taken near Seabrook, a small town on the bay about twenty-five miles north of Galveston.[157] Shortly after their indictment, both men were found guilty on seven counts of conspiracy to smuggle illegal alcohol through the Gulf of Mexico.[158] These charges essentially caused the demise of the Downtown Gang, which eliminated local competition for the Beach Gang, as well as competition for Sam and Rose Maceo.

Musey was sentenced to three years and six months in prison. However, he had fled Galveston even before the indictments were returned. He was reportedly seen taking a motorboat in order to catch a steamer.[159] From there, he fled to Canada, specifically Montreal. In his absence, as well as that of Nounes, Musey put a man by the name of Marvin J. "Big Jim" Clark in charge of the Downtown Gang's activities, subject to instructions from Musey in Canada. Unfortunately, Musey and Big Jim were unable to agree on a few details. This led to betrayal, deceit and the end of the Downtown Gang.[160]

Clark had his own alcohol-smuggling operations in Montreal to continue handling. Overall, Musey was unsatisfied with the way Clark neglected the Downtown Gang's business on Galveston Island. Supposedly, there might have been a woman involved, although there is no clear indication of who she may have been. Whatever the cause for the tension between the two men, Big Jim betrayed Musey by providing the Maceos with the opportunity to retaliate against Musey for his past indiscretions; that is, for previously having intercepted the brothers' alcohol shipments.[161]

After waiting for so long, the circumstances were right for Sam and Rose Maceo to act. Their next move ultimately won them complete control of Galveston's illegal activities. Before Clark abandoned the island city for good, he informed the Beach Gang about one of Musey's shipments that was scheduled to arrive. Thereafter, the Beach Gang promptly intercepted Musey's transports and stole over $200,000 worth of liquor.[162] Unfortunately for Musey, reports at that time indicate he was still on the run, which made it difficult for him to defend his territory and shipments.[163]

Ultimately, this served as a lesson to Musey. Nonetheless, after the Maceo brothers stole liquor from the Downtown Gang, tensions were running even higher than normal in Galveston. At first, it appeared that Musey would not retaliate. The two gangs were even, after all, but all was not good on the island. About three weeks after the Maceos stole Musey's shipment, a shootout occurred downtown on Tremont Street that involved members from both of Galveston's crime groups. It resulted in the deaths of members from each gang.[164]

This particular event removed one man from Galveston's underworld permanently. The local newspaper stated that Clarence Gregory died of multiple gunshot wounds at John Sealy Hospital. The two men initially charged for the shooting were Theodore "Fatty" Owens and James "Jimmie" Crabb. Owens was convicted and sentenced to two years of imprisonment. Another gentleman, Mitchell Frankovich, suffered a minor chest wound from the gunfight.[165] Upon release, Frankovich faced charges for "rudely displaying a pistol and discharging firearms in the city limits."[166]

The significance of this shooting is how it helped Sam and Rose Maceo. As already emphasized, events such as this shootout helped to eliminate competition. This enabled the Maceos to advance closer to the top. The man who died as a result of bullet wounds would never cause the Maceos any more trouble. Furthermore, the men who had charges filed against them would not be a threat as long as they were on trial or in prison. While the justice system acted to detain the men in order to decrease the threat against the general public, the Maceos benefited from the decreased threat to their illegitimate ambitions.

By this point in time, the Maceo brothers had progressed to nearly the top echelon in Galveston's organized crime scene. Nevertheless, Voight still had control over the Beach Gang, and the Maceos did not want to step on any toes. By then, the two brothers had expanded their business and owned a couple of clubs near the Seawall. Voight owned a club as well. However, he kept his business in downtown Galveston. Voight's downtown place was called the De Luxe Club. He also owned the Modern Vending Company, which provided gambling paraphernalia to other local businesses.[167] The Maceos were initially respectful of Voight's prior claim, never openly crossing into the original gang leader's downtown territory.

In 1925, the Maceo brothers finally carefully approached Voight regarding the De Luxe Club. Sam and Rose had discovered a minute detail that would possibly help them take that top position once and for all. The Maceos found that Voight did not own the property where his club was located. He actually leased the building. Therefore Sam reached out to the owner and made a deal on the property. Prudently, the two brothers also received Voight's blessing prior to having the property transferred to their ownership, while Quinn became their partner in developing a new club.

Essentially, Voight voluntarily stepped back from his position as a leader.[168] Thus, by the mid-1920s, Sam and Rose Maceo were in a position from which they controlled much of Galveston's illegal activity. As mentioned, the brothers basically did this openly. Local law enforcement officials knew what was occurring on the island. Yet because the community obviously benefited from such activities, a moral gray area existed. Perhaps the Maceos' rackets seemed inappropriate in other cities, but in Galveston, they were accepted. Although there were many factors affecting this attitude on the island, the greatest would most likely have been the diverse population dependent on tourism. The evolving makeup of the population created a moral gray area. The Maceos used this to their advantage.

THE HOLLYWOOD DINNER CLUB AND OTHER EARLY ESTABLISHMENTS

In 1921, shortly after the Maceos' first deal with Dutch Voight and Ollie Quinn, Sam and Rose gave up working as barbers for good. After working for low incomes for so long, the opportunity they earned by hiding liquor under Rose's house was extremely appealing. Therefore, the two men opened up a "soda shop." This business was just a front for the Maceos to continue selling bootlegged liquor.[169] Before long, the brothers advanced to a broader field: they expanded to gambling and alcohol under one roof.

The first club opened by Sam and Rose was called the Chop Suey Café.[170] The club's grand opening was scheduled for the evening of October 18, 1922. Chop Suey was located on a fishing pier at Twenty-first Street. It advertised music, dancing and fine dining.[171] This advertisement, of course, did not mention the gambling and alcohol that also would be offered behind the scenes. This location would become one of the most famous in Galveston, although not always under the same name.[172]

The year 1926 became an especially successful one for Sam and Rose. After changing the name of Chop Suey Café to Maceo's Grotto, the two brothers opened a new location: the Hollywood Dinner Club. The opening was scheduled for June 9, 1926, and was one of the largest and most anticipated events of the year. At a cost of $50,000 (almost a $700,000 value today), the club was designed to accommodate a total of five hundred guests. This large venue impressively sold out for its opening night almost a week in advance. In addition, on the Sunday before the actual opening of the club, Sam opened the doors for a sneak peak to the local Galvestonians, and this event alone attracted over five thousand curious guests.[173]

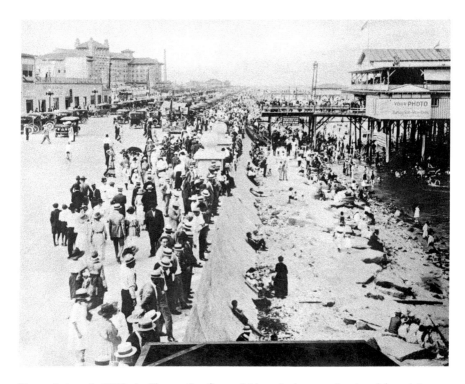

Pictured above in 1909, the Twenty-first Street fishing pier became the site of four clubs after the Maceos' procurement in 1922. *Courtesy of the Rosenberg Library.*

The Hollywood Dinner Club was located at Sixty-first Street and Avenue S in Galveston.[174] It was reportedly the first air-conditioned nightclub in the United States. The décor was elaborate, down to the crystal chandeliers. The club offered first-class cuisine, the nation's best entertainers and, of course, illegal gambling and alcohol. The operation was predicted to be "one of the finest and most elaborate [clubs] in the South."[175] Perhaps it lived up to these expectations.

The Maceo brothers were known for not only providing the finest food and illegal gambling and drinks but also the finest entertainment. Local historian Frank E. Chalfant, an expert on the gambling industry in Galveston, listed the typical entertainment at the Hollywood Dinner Club. He explained that popular entertainers and musicians were often invited to the club, including Frank Sinatra, Sophie Tucker, Joe E. Lewis, the Ritz Brothers, Peggy Lee, Phil Harris, Henry Busse, Isham Jones, Bob Crosby, Ben Pollack, Guy Lombardo, Ted Mack, Jimmy Dorsey, Ted Weems, Shep Fields, Ray Noble and Freddy Martin.[176] This list, of course, included great singers and the leaders of some

HOLLYWOOD
Dinner Club
GALVESTON

61ST AND S ROAD   PHONE GALVESTON 1022

By Popular Demand
SAM MACEO PRESENTS
HENRY BUSSE
and His Famous 17-Piece Dance Band

Also

The South's Finest Floor Show

No Advance in Price Scale

Cover Charge Saturdays, $1.65; Other Nights, 75c
Phone Galveston 1022 for Choice Table Reservations

The Hollywood Dinner Club was a predecessor to the Balinese Room, offering only the finest food, décor and entertainment. *Courtesy of the* Galveston Daily News.

of the most famous big bands; after all, the Hollywood Dinner Club boasted that it provided the best musical entertainment available.

It was said that few celebrities ever passed through the island without meeting Sam Maceo. He invited them to his clubs and sometimes even provided them with a suite at the Galvez Hotel.[177] With promises of only first-class cuisine, gambling and some of the nation's finest entertainers, the opening of the Hollywood Dinner Club appealed to more than the just the island's locals.[178] Reservations for its opening night were made by social elites from several Texas cities, such as Houston, Dallas and San Antonio.[179] Prior to its grand opening, the island's local newspaper announced that

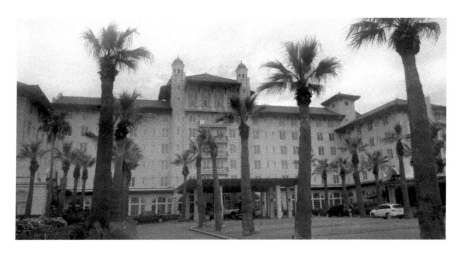

The Galvez Hotel was directly across Seawall Boulevard from the Balinese Room and was frequented by many of the club's top entertainers. *Courtesy of Amanda Belshaw.*

stage director George McQueen had already booked the club's first featured talents. McQueen promised big names such as Coster and Rich of Chicago, Virginia Cooper, the Brock (Brox) Sisters and Gilbert Wells, vaudeville partner of Florence Brady.[180] When the club opened its doors on June 9, 1926, Harry Samuels's dance orchestra provided the opening act.[181]

The Hollywood Dinner Club opened for each summer season for over a decade. Typically, Sam would open his club doors in early May and close them at the beginning of September. In 1927, the club opened on May 11, under the close scrutiny of the Texas Rangers and their ally, Texas attorney general Claude Pollard, Nounes's nemesis.[182] In the middle of this summer season, the club had an injunction filed against it on the suspicion that it was not just a country club, as had been previously claimed.[183]

Soon after the injunction was filed, Pollard asked for a forfeiture of the club's charter on the grounds that Sam Maceo was running a gambling establishment. Overall, the publicity was too much for Sam, who only wanted to provide locals and tourists with entertainment and memorable evenings.[184] In order to avoid additional negative publicity, he chose to end his second season with the club early. Although it is unclear how, Sam did find a way to have the doors reopen the next season.

When the Hollywood Dinner Club was closed between seasons, Sam Maceo allowed other major events to take place there. For example, the annual Red Cross Dance took place there every December, beginning in 1933.[185] Also the Maceos frequently planned an elaborate New Year's celebration at the club. Community members could, at any time, rent the club for private events. That is what occasionally occurred throughout the slow seasons. The Hollywood Dinner Club continued to open each season until 1940, when the Texas Rangers finally padlocked the doors after an investigation.[186]

During the Hollywood Dinner Club's open season, Sam continued to have only the best entertainment scheduled. For example, on April 18, 1934, the opening act was Guy Lombardo and his Royal Canadians. This was the first time that Lombardo played in the state of Texas. Moreover, before opening for the club, it was reported that the band had only performed in New York, Los Angeles, Chicago and Cleveland that year.[187] Still, Lombardo was not the only big name performer who became associated with Galveston. All of the Maceo brothers' establishments regularly featured nationally recognized names, as well as some of the finest regional and local talent.

The summer after Lombardo's acclaimed debut in Galveston, Ben Bernie and his orchestra performed at the Hollywood Dinner Club. The band was originally scheduled to perform for only three weeks. However, there was an extremely high demand for more opportunities to see Bernie and his band. Therefore, Sam extended their contract for a total of six weeks.[188] Furthermore, Galvestonians started off the New Year with Gus Arnheim in 1935. He was scheduled to perform with his orchestra at two of the Maceos' establishments, the Hollywood Dinner Club and the Sui Jen Café (originally the Chop Suey Café and then Maceo's Grotto), throughout the holiday celebrations.[189] Consequently, many tourists did not exclusively visit the island for the beach.

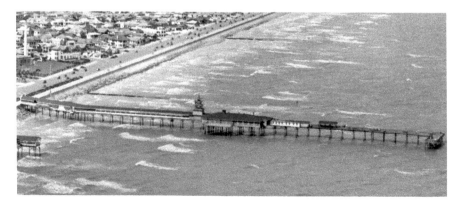

Before the establishment became known as the Balinese Room, Twenty-first and Seawall was home to the Sui Jen Café, an oriental-themed restaurant. *Courtesy of the Rosenberg Library.*

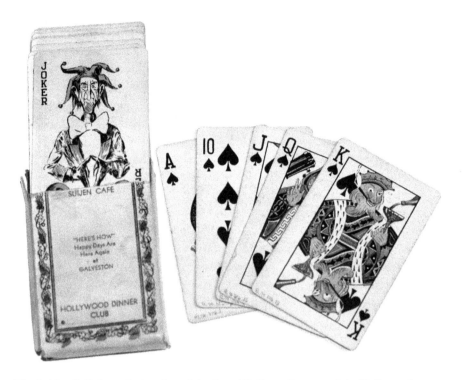

The Sui Jen Café, later the location of the famed Balinese Room, and the Hollywood Dinner Club are advertised on these playing cards. *Courtesy of the Rosenberg Library.*

In addition to housing an array of entertainment businesses under a single roof, Sam Maceo also offered another novel business idea. He arranged to have his popular entertainment shared across the town. The Hollywood Dinner Club offered the first "remote radio broadcast." The *Galveston Daily News* announced that Sam had spent $30,000 on a contract with Thomas Goggan and Brother Piano Company. This partnership provided the Maceo brothers with the instruments and other equipment to broadcast the live entertainment of the club three nights a week on the KFUL radio station. Sam also invested to have an elaborate wire system installed so that the Maceos' clubs and restaurants downtown could enjoy the top musicians.

Overall, the Maceos had created a substantial business for themselves. The pair worked perfectly together. Rose was tough and smart. He worked as a bodyguard or enforcer. Sam, on the other hand, was charming and good-looking. He built effective relationships and served as the public figure for the Maceos' criminal operations.[190] Together, the brothers had become the most prominent figures in the island city's illicit activities.

In 1928, the Maceos remodeled the former Chop Suey Café. The location on Twenty-first and Seawall was then known as Maceo's Grotto. Unfortunately, the grotto did not survive long. The next year, the grotto was subjected to a raid by state law enforcement agents and was closed down due to liquor and gambling violations. After being forced to close the club, the Maceo brothers sold the property to a third party. Someone else owned the pier until it was damaged by a hurricane in 1932. Thereafter, the brothers bought the property back and reopened it as the Sui Jen Café. Under the new name, the building was returned to its Asian décor and cuisine.

It is rumored that after Japan bombed Pearl Harbor and the United States entered World War II, Sam and Rose Maceo decided to remodel the Sui Jen Café again, to eliminate any potential associations to be made between the war and the atmosphere in their club.[191] On the other hand, the dates do not suggest this, for Pearl Harbor was bombed on December 7, 1941. Originally, the remodeled club, renamed the Balinese Room, was scheduled to open on New Year's Eve in 1941. If the devastating attack had influenced the design of the building, Sam would not have had a sufficient amount of time to prepare for the opening. Conversely, as local history columnist William Cherry has suggested, the attack on Pearl Harbor may have actually delayed the opening of the new club.[192]

Cherry states that the Balinese Room had been constructed by early December. Sam and Rose had friends and family come to the location to appraise the new design and possibly provide suggestions. However, the night that his close associates and relatives arrived, the radio reported the Japanese attack. As the guests recalled, Sam went to the bar and sat by himself whilst having a drink, absorbing the news. Then, as family and friends recall, Sam went into hiding, isolating himself over the next couple of weeks. When he reemerged, he stated that he did not like the bandstand and wanted it completely reconstructed. Cherry states that this is the reason the club did not open on New Year's Eve as planned. Instead, after the bandstand was redesigned, the Balinese Room officially opened on January 17, 1942.[193]

Undaunted by the complications attending the opening of the Balinese Room, Sam began planning the next phase for the Maceo business on the pier. Then, on a trip to Tennessee, he saw the Hotel Claridge in Memphis. He felt inspired by the design and demanded to know who had created the plan for the building. He discovered that a man by the name of Virgil Quadri, a Massachusetts Institute of Technology graduate, had designed the hotel, so he quickly boarded a train to Chicago to locate Quadri. Together, Quadri and a New York architect designed the new club for the

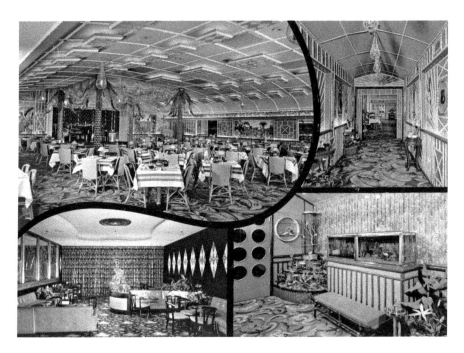

The Balinese Room was known for its extravagant décor, fine dining and big entertainers. It attracted high rollers from all over the country. *Courtesy of the Rosenberg Library.*

Maceos at Twenty-first and Seawall, which would continue to be known as the Balinese Room.[194]

The Balinese Room became a nationally recognized name. It ultimately replaced the Hollywood Dinner Club, which closed in the late 1930s. As they had done at the Hollywood Dinner Club, the Maceos allowed no less than the best to perform in their Balinese Room night after night. Examples of such entertainers included the Marx Brothers, Frank Sinatra, Tony Bennett, Guy Lombardo and the Three Stooges, as well as many more who were just as popular. The Balinese Room provided more than just the biggest entertainers. The nightclub also welcomed the "highest-rolling gamblers." And the Maceo brothers always provided an escort home to those gamblers who won big.[195]

The Maceos did not believe it was good business to have locals gambling in their clubs. Therefore, they targeted high rollers from out of town. According to Robert Nieman, the brothers understood that their illicit business ventures would succeed only as long as Galvestonians allowed them to do so.[196] Therefore, Sam and Rose did not want the citizens of the island coming into their clubs and losing money. That would be, Sam believed, the quickest way to lose the residents' support for their illegal activities.

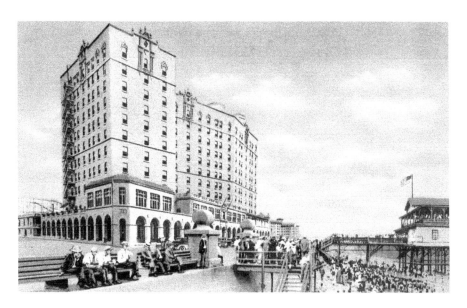

The Buccaneer Hotel penthouse suite served as a luxurious home for Sam Maceo for several years until he built a home in Galveston. *Courtesy of the Rosenberg Library.*

As mentioned earlier, the Maceo brothers eventually owned outright or were partners in more than sixty establishments on Galveston Island and on the nearby mainland. In addition to the Hollywood Dinner Club and the Balinese Room, the brothers had many other clubs and restaurants. These included the Studio Lounge, the Oyster Bar, the Streamline Dinner Club (near Algoa) and the Fish Room. Also, as mentioned, the two brothers had slot machines throughout the island's businesses. They leased the machines through Gulf Properties, which replaced Quinn's Modern Vending Company after the brothers squeezed him out. Through this company, slot machines were placed in ordinary businesses all across the island.[197]

One of the additional clubs the brothers established was the Turf Athletic Club. This club served as the unofficial headquarters for the Maceos' crime syndicate.[198] This club, like the Hollywood Dinner Club and the Balinese Room, was decorated extravagantly. After local Isaac Kempner visited the Turf Athletic Club, he reported to his daughter, "Nowhere this side of Hollywood has there been more lavish or lurid décor. It is on the whole in good taste."[199] Furthermore, at the Turf Athletic Club, sports betting took place. Bets could be placed on baseball games and horse races—the latter of the two being the only thing on which Sam Maceo reportedly bet.[200]

BEYOND ORGANIZED CRIME:
PERSONAL CONTRIBUTIONS TO THE ISLAND

Beyond the obvious assets Sam and Rose Maceo brought to Galveston Island with them—an understanding and appreciation for organized crime—there was something else that ensured their success. As the brothers became leaders in Galveston's underworld, they never gave up their support for the people who lived in the island city. They continued to offer businesses that, although illegal, would benefit and interest the citizens. Plus, they continued to give to the community. Thus, the growth of the island empire exceeded anyone's expectations of a couple of barbers.

The Maceo brothers positively affected the island overall. When the rest of the country was experiencing the Great Depression, it is said that Galveston was untouched by the unfortunate economic circumstances. Nieman wrote, "There was a worldwide depression everywhere but in Galveston, where money flowed as freely as the ocean that lapped its shores."[201] Furthermore, it is argued that the island's hotels were booked full of guests throughout the year and that no bank shut down throughout this turbulent time.[202]

In addition to the general effect Sam and Rose had on the economy and social life of Galveston Island, the brothers also had a direct effect on many local families. For example, they helped put one man's children through college. That man, Mike Mitchell, was a father to four children. Naturally, Mitchell wanted to be able to provide his children with a substantial education, but he also knew he would not be able to pay for four college tuitions on his meager income. Therefore, Sam offered to help pay for each child's college education.

According to Mitchell's son George, his father was never able to pay these loans back to Sam in full. Nonetheless, Sam never demanded repayment for these loans. That is just how Sam was. In 1951, local writer Edwin E. Llewellyn wrote an article remembering Sam. He stated that Sam never demanded the repayment of his loans. Instead, he would tell people, "Someday when you run across somebody who is really in need or is sick, take the money and give him a helping hand."[203]

Of course, the Mitchell family never forgot how Sam helped them. Because of his financial assistance, all four of the children were able to attend college. Specifically, due to Sam's graciousness, George was able to earn his degree in petroleum engineering. As a way to thank Sam years later and to continue the Maceo family's legacy on Galveston Island, George returned to build Sam's San Luis Hotel. This was a hotel plan that Sam

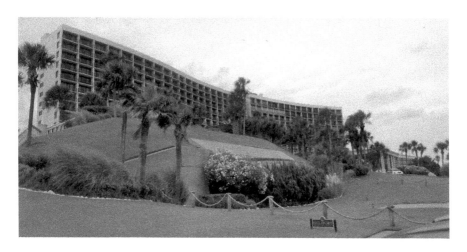

San Luis Hotel was supposedly based on a plan Sam Maceo had abandoned years earlier and completed as a way to thank and remember Maceo. *Courtesy of Amanda Belshaw.*

had abandoned years earlier after a protest from the Moody family. Because of Sam's generosity to a needy father, over fifty years later, Galvestonians finally got their hotel.[204]

Galveston locals also witnessed the kindness of Sam Maceo in 1947. That spring, Texas City, one of Galveston's neighboring port cities, suffered one of the deadliest accidents in American history. After a series of five explosions, over five hundred people were left dead, and the city was heavily damaged. Sam's son and namesake reported in 2007, just six months before his own death, that his father hosted several benefits for the victims of Texas City. He brought in famous entertainers and raised large amounts of money to help fund the recovery of the shattered community.[205] This sort of generosity was not an aberration in Sam's character. One resident reported the brothers "gave truckloads of cash to charities, especially the Catholic Church. Subsequently, Galveston liked the Maceo brothers as much as the brothers liked Galveston."[206]

Rose, on the other hand, was tough. He was both feared and respected. It is also said that he was the true head of the Maceo family and their operations.[207] Because of this stature, Rose served as the muscle of the family and enforced the rules of the game. As previously explained, it was rumored that Rose's first wife and her lover were murdered, and their bodies were found floating in Galveston Bay.[208] For many residents, this local story, whether true or not, provided an idea of what their fates would be if they crossed Rose. And though many residents suspected that he might have been

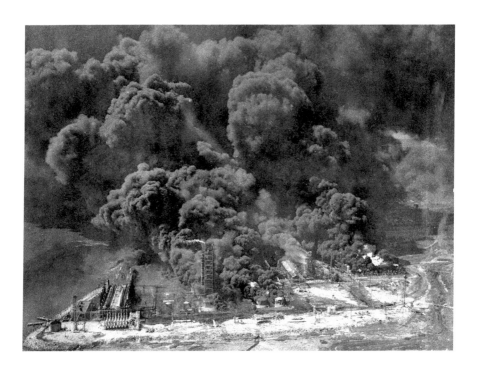

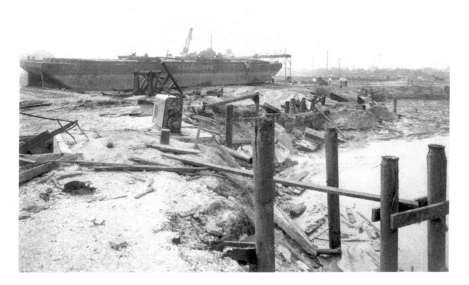

This page: The Texas City explosion remains the deadliest industrial accident in United States history. Several events were held throughout Galveston in the weeks that followed in order to raise money. *Courtesy of the Moore Memorial Public Library.*

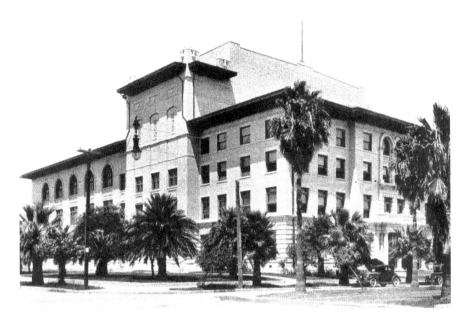

The Galveston Municipal Auditorium was used to host a fundraising event after the Texas City explosion in 1942. *Courtesy of the Rosenberg Library.*

the one to blame for a few crimes on the island, Rose was never convicted of any crime. Nor was his brother Sam convicted.

In addition to his muscle and ambition, Rose also provided another asset to the family: enforcement operations. He created the Night Riders.[209] Rose's Night Riders served as an informal police force on Galveston Island. It was reported that during the Maceos' reign from the 1920s to the 1950s, the island remained crime free. No one needed to lock their doors during this time period. Nor did the citizens fear walking through the streets at night. It is even reported that the family bookkeeper, Sam "Books" Serio, would walk to the local bank carrying up to a million dollars with no protection. As historian Gary Cartwright dryly explained, "They ran a clean fame in a clean town, and anybody who didn't like it slept with the fishes."[210]

When all the circumstances in Galveston are examined, it is understandable that there was such tolerance for illicit activities. Galveston's historical factors collided with the social realities of the early 1900s. The result was a unique atmosphere: a moral gray area. However, Sam's contributions to the community made the Maceo brothers' presence that much more compelling. Plus, given Rose's reputation, it is likely that each resident on the island felt safer with the illegal activities than he would have without them. For anyone who knew, Galveston during the reign of the Maceos in many ways bore a strong resemblance to the Sicily they had left behind.

CHALLENGING THE EMPIRE

LEGAL TROUBLES AND FEDERAL INVESTIGATIONS

Although Galveston locals largely accepted the Maceo brothers' vice activities, there was a small group of conservative Protestants and Methodists who felt that their city required a legal intervention from an outside, and detached, agency. However, these individuals were few in number compared to those who not only endorsed the activities but also indulged in them. Nevertheless, the Maceos' influence relied on local acceptance. Toward the end of the 1930s, the complaints from the religious conservatives reached the governor's office in Austin, Texas, which brought legal repercussions that shook the Maceos' empire in the "Free State of Galveston."

In the 1935 Texas governor's race, James V. Allred was elected after receiving 93 percent of the votes.[211] Prior to taking his seat as governor, Allred had served as the state's attorney general. As such, Galveston's illicit activities had already been brought to his attention. In 1934, Allred received correspondence alluding to the "vice conditions" in the island city.[212] Thereafter, and during his gubernatorial campaign, he emphasized the need for control over Texas's persistent underworld. Galveston was merely one of several locations throughout the state that participated in vice activities. It is obvious in a review of Allred's papers that the same fight was being fought in other Texas cities, such as Houston, Dallas, Fort Worth, San Antonio, El Paso and San Augustine. But Galveston became a top priority for Allred.

As described in previous chapters, Galveston had been an open city for several years. However, the times were changing, and there was a small group of oppositionists forming. Though it was a small portion of the island city's population, Galveston's underworld was beginning to face a local backlash. As stated, this was largely due to a growing number of highly religious and conservative residents. These individuals believed that such activities were shameful. Moreover, many of the local churches disapproved of the sinful lifestyle.

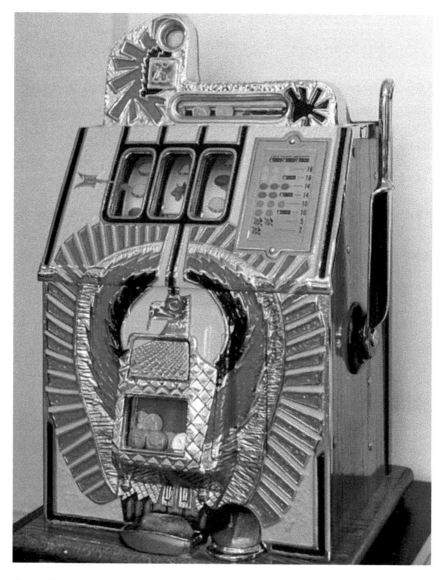

Pictured is an example of the type of gambling paraphernalia the Texas Rangers discovered and destroyed in the 1957 raids. *Courtesy of the Library of Congress.*

In one letter to Governor Allred, a gentleman wrote about the hundreds of slot machines found throughout the island, stating that they were located in "most places except the churches." Furthermore, he spoke of liquor in various shops and private rooms found at the back of several establishments, which were regularly visited by young men and women. The man declared, "GALVESTON IS A FIRST CLASS HELL ON EARTH!" At the end of the letter, the writer stated that he would not sign his name "for fear of reprisals from the [gangsters]."[213]

Similarly, Reverend Charles D. Snowden of Grace Church in Alvin, Texas, wrote to Allred to thank him for his efforts to subdue the various illegal establishments located along the thirty-two miles of highway between Galveston and Alvin.[214] The treasurer of the First Baptist Church in Galveston also wrote to the governor, stating that he understood he had made a movement against such activities in other major cities but declaring that Galveston especially required his attention.[215] There was an obvious trend in the incoming correspondence from Galvestonians concerned about the island's underworld. It is important to note again, almost every letter included in Allred's correspondence came from active members or leaders in local religious establishments.

After receiving various reports regarding the illegal activities continuing to occur in Galveston, Governor Allred elected to investigate the claims. Prior to his interest in the matter, law enforcement raids rarely occurred on the island. When they did occur, the Maceo family was not the target of the raids. Instead, the "independent slot machine owners" were the target of the raids.[216] According to one estimate, there were about 1,500 slot machines on the island.[217] Therefore, raids against the "independent" owners did not yield a significant amount of paraphernalia.

Soon after his election as governor, Allred asked for a private investigation to be conducted in Galveston. He was particularly interested in Sam Maceo and Ralph Hicks "in regard to reported alleged conspiracy to operate gambling establishments in the State of Texas."[218] Although a report on the "confidential investigation" cannot be found in his papers, Allred's actions throughout subsequent years indicate that the investigation yielded enough evidence to confirm the claims from the conservative residents of Galveston and thus to compel him to act.

Although the cries for help came from a very small portion of Galveston citizens, it was enough to gain the attention of the governor and thus state law enforcement agencies. Likewise, there were a few other circumstances that earned the island some negative attention. Additional negative light was shone on the island city through a few critical magazine and newspaper articles. By the late 1930s, Galveston's crime syndicate was under increasing pressure. Despite the Maceo brothers' best efforts to disguise their illicit businesses, the true nature of their operation on the island was slowly being revealed to outsiders such as Allred, who ordered state officials into action.

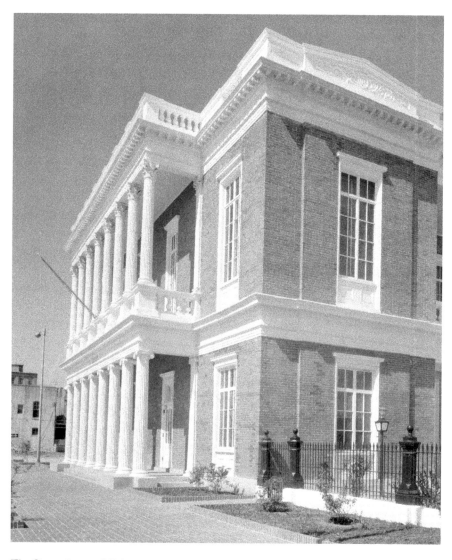

The Customhouse of Galveston County was built in the nineteenth century. In 1917, the second floor was renovated and provided federal courtrooms. *Courtesy of the Library of Congress.*

This series of events led to an investigation of Sam Maceo and his potential involvement in the drug trade. As the decade was coming to an end, Sam faced his first charges as a criminal from the federal courts. The case was highly publicized with updates in newspapers from all over the country. However, his most lucrative business, the Balinese Room, was yet to be established. It would be almost two more decades before state investigators would be able to penetrate the club's elaborate alarm system and bring down the infamous establishment, as well as the rest of the island's rackets.

MACEO'S FIGHT AGAINST DRUG CHARGES

As mentioned, Galveston's rackets were gaining new negative attention in the late 1930s, largely from outside sources. One example of this was an article published in the *American Detective*. The article discussed the illegal activities on the island, arguing that not only were they were not advantageous to the community, but they were in fact harmful, especially to the younger generation. Furthermore, the article discussed how the Maceo brothers had become involved in the transportation of illegal drugs and the repercussions on Galveston that resulted from this new racket.[219]

For example, there was a series of murders that were blamed on the growing Galveston underworld. Although the Maceos were not directly tied to any of the deaths, their involvement in the criminal world was suspected to have indirectly caused the violence. One incident was the murder of a young woman named Pauline Johnson. Johnson had previously served as an informant in a robbery case. Friends said Johnson suspected she had a target on her back—she was afraid she would be killed for her involvement in the case. Then, one morning, her body was found in a ditch between Houston and Galveston. Her head had been hit repeatedly, resulting in it being essentially crushed.[220]

In addition to Johnson's murder, an individual known only as Junkie Joe was found dead along Alvin Road. He had been stabbed in the heart and cheek. The *American Detective* article blamed the network of criminal individuals connected to the Maceos for these unfortunate deaths. Particularly, the article blamed the drug trade for causing the rise in violence throughout the 1930s. This added to speculation regarding what was actually occurring on the island. Although Sam Maceo always denied involvement in the drug trade, this provided the general public with potentially new—and disturbing—information about the Maceo family's activities.[221]

According to the article, after Prohibition was revoked in 1933, the "Wop Mob" and "Jew Mob," two groups in New York that dominated the drug trade in the United States, recognized the potential in Galveston's location. Once again, the island provided an ideal geographic position for illegal smuggling and trading, just as it did for Jean Lafitte in the early nineteenth century and to the island's gangs throughout the 1920s. In addition to recruiting Galveston gangsters, the New York groups included Dallas, Houston and Fort Worth in their expansion of business.[222]

The men who operated from these four locations made up what was referred to as the inside ring. According to the article, for four years, surveillance was focused on the Big Four, one of whom was Sam Maceo. In the end, Sam's arrest was highly publicized. One of the many pictures posted in the article painted him as a crook, an image not often portrayed by the local newspapers.[223] The ensuing case lasted six years.

The article shed such negative light that supposedly Sam Maceo tried to eliminate the evidence. The accession record at Rosenberg Library in Galveston states that the donor of the magazine article that appeared in *American Detective* informed the library staff that the article was extremely rare. According to the donor, Sam attempted to buy every copy of the magazine in Galveston and New Orleans. As a result, not many articles survived and not many people read how the Maceo family may have become involved with one of the most extensive drug-smuggling rings.

The actual prosecution of Sam Maceo began with his arrest on October 6, 1937. The newspaper in Mexia, Texas, reported that Maceo was one of twenty-four persons arrested by federal agents in raids conducted simultaneously in Galveston and Houston. "The raids coincided with other raids in New York and several other cities a[s] government agents swooped down on alleged members of an international drug-smuggling ring."[224] The warrant for arrest was issued based on the eyewitness testimony of a federal narcotics agent, Emory W. Clapper.[225]

Clapper testified he saw Sam Maceo and another defendant, Alphonse Attardi, a mobster from New York, enter a residence in Galveston on September 8, 1937. Maceo and his defense counsel argued that it was a case of mistaken identity and presented the courtroom with a man who resembled him. Upon being asked if he may have falsely identified Maceo, Clapper admitted it was possible "if he had not seen his face."[226] However, the defense counsel argued that Maceo was not in Galveston the night he

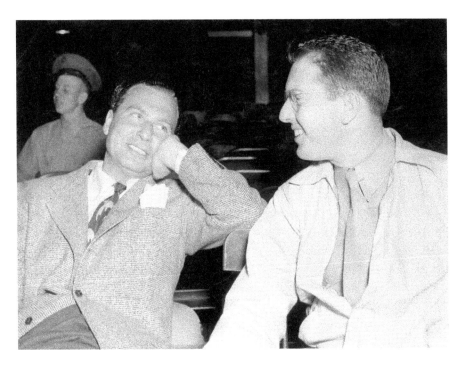

In addition to performing at the Balinese Room, Phil Harris (center) also served as an alibi for Sam Maceo when he was faced with federal charges. *Courtesy of the Rosenberg Library.*

was identified as a visitor to the Galveston home; he was in Dallas.[227] Phil Harris, the famed orchestra player who admittedly had been a guest of the Maceo brothers in their clubs, later testified that Sam Maceo was with him in Dallas.[228]

The various defendants involved in the Sam Maceo narcotics case were charged with "conspiracy to violate the tariff act, the import and export act and the Harrison narcotics act."[229] Because New York was used as a central location in the trafficking of narcotics, federal prosecutors intended to file for a removal and try the defendants in a New York courtroom.[230] However, removal relied on the admissibility of sufficient evidence—something the defense was arguing the government did not have.

Sam Maceo's attorney, Louis J. Dibrell, and the other defense attorneys argued that the charges relied on a large amount of evidence that was not admissible in court. Clapper, the federal agent who had identified Maceo as an involved party, informed the court that there was substantial evidence collected through the use of wire-tapping the defendants' telephone lines.[231] However, prior to Maceo's trial, the United States Supreme Court had ruled that the wire-tapping procedure was invalid.[232] Furthermore, Clapper testified that he had purchased three hundred ounces of narcotics from the Big Four distributors in Texas, but he lacked the evidence to tie the drugs to New York.[233]

On January 24, 1938, the ruling from the federal removal hearing, which had been pending for over three months, finally came. United States commissioner George W. Coltzer placed Sam Maceo, as well as twelve other defendants, in jail until their removal to New York to stand trial.[234] One of the other defendants was Biaggio Angelica. Angelica served as one of Sam Maceo's subordinates, stationed in nearby Houston.[235] Immediately after hearing the results of the hearing, Maceo's defense counsel, as well as that for Angelica, applied for writs of habeas corpus.[236] However, Federal District judge Thomas W. Davidson, a former lieutenant governor of Texas, upheld the previous decision for removal. The defense responded with a notice to appeal the decision.[237] In July, the district court decision was again upheld. The Fifth Circuit Court of Appeals in New Orleans placed Maceo in the custody of a federal marshal until his removal to New York.[238]

In the final decision to uphold the decision for Sam Maceo's removal, the Court of Appeals argued that his testimony consisted of little more than denying his involvement in the drug-smuggling ring and denying his identity as one of the defendants. The court added, "Aside from the question of identity, which seems to us to be clearly established, the evidence in this case, when boiled down, consists of the indictment on the one hand and the relator's general denial on the other." Aside from the initial indictment, the government had not shown probable cause. However, Maceo also failed to provide any evidence to suggest he was innocent, other than his word. Therefore, the Circuit Court relied on the previous opinion of Commissioner Coltzer.[239]

It is very likely that the defense team suspected the results for Sam Maceo's case would be better if he was tried in the state of Texas. Maceo was a familiar name in the southern state. Local newspapers throughout the state frequently reported on his charities, big name entertainment and club openings. Aside from the highly religious residents, Texans in general apparently favored Maceo. Therefore, removal to the Northeast—a place miles from his home, where most people did not recognize the Maceo name—was likely to be unfavorable to the gangster. Perhaps that is why the defense fought so long and hard against removal.

After a long legal fight, Sam Maceo was remanded without bail to the Galveston County jail, where he was required to stay until his appearance in a New York courtroom.[240] Although his trial was not scheduled to begin until November 1938, he was extradited to New York in late August.[241] Upon his arrival, he again pleaded innocent.[242] He continued to maintain his innocence until the end of the narcotics trials four years later.

Prior to the start of Sam Maceo's trial, a number of individuals had already pleaded guilty or been convicted in related prosecutions. One of these was Angelica, whose defense counsel similarly tried to fight his removal to New York. Angelica was sentenced by a federal judge in Houston to serve ten years in prison and pay a $2,000 fine. The same week that his sentence was announced, eight other individuals were also sentenced in the narcotics case. Overall, it was arguably the largest narcotics case in the Galveston area.[243] It was estimated that the operations "handled between $5,000,000 and $25,000,000 worth of narcotics during a two-year period."[244] Over the next months, the federal courts learned that the huge ring was actually even larger than they had initially imagined.

In November 1938, Sam Maceo's trial did not begin as originally planned. Little news regarding the case was released through the winter months. Then, on January 15, 1939, additional persons were indicted for involvement in the narcotics case. The group was indicted for operating a drug-smuggling ring out of New Orleans and having "contacts" with the international drug-smuggling operations with which Maceo was suspected of being involved. This event brought the total number of indictments from the original 88 to 103.[245]

By February 1939, Sam Maceo had finally been released under a $10,000 bond by the New York court. Then assistant United States attorney Joseph Martin announced that he was unsure when the Maceo trial would begin. According to Martin, the trial would remain pending "until after the United States Circuit Court of Appeals has acted upon appeals of codefendants in the case who were tried last fall."[246] Of the eighty-eight persons originally indicted, forty-five went to trial. Of those who went to trial, forty-two were convicted. A San Antonio newspaper reported that "two were appealing their convictions with arguments based on the defense claim of technical weaknesses in the indictment."[247] The decision in these appeals was important in determining if Maceo would be brought to court on the original indictment or if a new indictment would be filed.

By the fall of 1939, Sam Maceo's trial was still on hold, pending a final decision on the appeals. One of the two appellants was Jerry Bruno. Bruno had originally been sentenced to two years in prison and a $5,000 fine. The Federal Circuit Court at New York upheld the original conviction. Upon receiving the decision, Bruno immediately appealed to the Supreme

Court.[248] Because of the importance that the Supreme Court's decision would have on the Maceo case, it was announced that the latter would remain in abeyance—a temporary suspension.[249] By September 1940, more than two years after Maceo's original indictment, the case was removed from the federal court calendar. Martin stated at that time that the case "might be tried some time later, or it might never come to trial."[250]

MACEO'S NARCOTICS CONSPIRACY TRIAL: DRUG PEDDLER OR FINE CITIZEN?

Toward the end of 1941, there was talk about Sam Maceo's case being placed back on the federal court calendar. The next spring, Edith A. Glannon was assigned as the prosecutor in the case.[251] A few months later, an official date was set for the case. After four years, Sam was finally required to stand trial in New York on September 16, 1942.[252] When the trial began, newspapers across Texas and the surrounding states covered the story. After such an extended abeyance, the Maceo case was highly anticipated and widely covered.

On September 22, 1942, Sam Maceo finally went to trial for his 1938 indictment for involvement in what was called one of the largest drug rings ever discovered.[253] In addition, Clapper, the federal narcotics agent who had originally identified Maceo as an involved party, also appeared in court to testify. In the early stages of the narcotics case, Clapper refused to provide details about what Maceo was doing when he was initially identified. He argued that the information was provided before a grand jury in New York and that "he was under oath not to divulge that testimony."[254] That information was never released in newspapers even after the case resumed in 1942. However, the agent *was* able to testify about what he witnessed when he presented himself as an interested customer in Galveston.

Clapper stated he had met a sailor while in Galveston in the summer of 1937. Soon after their meeting, the sailor accompanied Clapper to a house in Galveston's red-light district. Clapper then described his encounter with Katherine Phillips. He explained that he told her he was interested in purchasing an ounce of heroin, and he assured Phillips that he would be back for more if he were satisfied with the product. Therefore, Phillips sold some heroin to him that initial evening. When Clapper returned later and informed her he would like to purchase a larger quantity, Phillips responded by saying she "represented the biggest drug syndicate in New York."[255]

Meeting Phillips proved to be vital to the government's case. Phillips set Clapper up with her New York connections, and soon after, Clapper met with "an Italian named 'Frank,' who offered to deliver heroin anywhere in whatever quantities wanted." Shortly after meeting this connection, Clapper had twenty-five ounces of heroin delivered to Waco, Texas.[256]

Phillips was also called to testify on behalf of the government. She stated that, in 1923, she had worked at a Galveston house of prostitution, and Sam Maceo had visited her frequently. By 1937, Phillips was the operator of her own prostitution house in the island city. In her testimony, she admitted involvement in the narcotics ring. She informed the courtroom that, on two different occasions, she had visited Maceo at his Turf Athletic Club to exchange money she had made from drug sales. She stated that the money had come from the women working for her in the prostitution house—those who worked for her regularly purchased the drugs.[257]

Sam Maceo's defense counsel tried hard to have the case against their client dismissed. In a push for dismissal, Maceo's attorney undermined each of the stories told by Clapper and Phillips. Regarding the former's identification of Maceo in Galveston on the night of September 8, 1937, Phil Harris testified in Maceo's favor. He declared that on the evening of the eighth, Maceo was with him in Dallas, as well as for the following two weeks. He stated, "I know that night well. It was the night my band closed an engagement at the Texas Centennial celebration at Dallas. Benny Goodman's band followed mine and Sam Maceo and I waited for Benny to open."[258]

In regard to Phillips's testimony, Maceo's counsel argued that her claims of knowing Sam Maceo as a "personal friend" were inaccurate. The defense stated that Phillips had previously testified she did not know Maceo. In a 1938 case, the defense claimed Phillips had testified that she operated her own drug business. In the previous case, when asked whether or not she knew Maceo, Phillips had declared, "I never knew him enough to recognize him until we were arrested. I knew him on the street, but not otherwise." Unfortunately for Maceo, the court upheld Phillips's right not to answer questions related to her earlier testimony for fear of self-incrimination.[259]

Although dismissal of the narcotics charges against Sam Maceo was not granted, the defense must have made a compelling case regarding his innocence or at least cast enough doubt on the government's evidence. It was announced later in the month that the federal jury could not agree on a verdict.[260] After further deliberation, Maceo was acquitted of all charges. However, the jury found his codefendant, Joseph Schipano, guilty.[261] Sam maintained before and after the verdict that he never dealt in drugs. From the beginning, he had argued, "I'm no angel but dealing in narcotics is 'just as foreign to me as it is to you.'"[262] It still remains unclear if Maceo was actually involved with the international drug-smuggling ring.

However, as previously pointed out, Angelica, Sam Maceo's codefendant, was a known associate of the Maceo family in their illicit operations. As mentioned, Angelica pleaded guilty in 1938 in a Houston court. For that conviction, he received ten years in jail. Then, in 1940, he received an additional eight years of imprisonment in a Galveston trial and another two years from the New York courts.[263] Each conviction was narcotics related. This begs the question, if Sam Maceo was not involved in the drug trade, why did one of his known associates receive three narcotics-related convictions?

Despite his luck in the narcotics case, his trial placed Sam Maceo on the radar of state and federal officials. If people did not know who he was and what he did before, they certainly must have after he was acquitted in 1942. Subsequent to his acquittal, there is clear evidence of increased surveillance and investigations from outside law enforcement agencies. It seems that there may have been more pressure on local officials to finally shut down the rackets in Galveston or bring down Maceo. However, in 1942, Sam received attention for more than his acquitted case. He had also recently opened the famed Balinese Room, which would serve as the main target of future investigations.

THE BALINESE ROOM: CHARGING DOWN RANGER RUN

The Balinese Room was in development for several years before becoming a nationally recognized club. As previously explained, the location went through four name changes and four redecorations before becoming infamous. After first being purchased by the Maceo brothers, the place became the Chop Suey Café. After renovations, the location off the Seawall was briefly known as Maceo's Grotto. Then, after being damaged by a hurricane in 1932, the location became known as the Sui Jen Café. Each one of these prior businesses was well known to the locals and tourists. However, it was not until 1942 that the location became the legendary Balinese Room.

The new club opened the same year that Sam Maceo was acquitted of all charges in his prolonged narcotics case. Even after all charges were dropped, Texas officials kept an eye on him. They suspected Maceo was involved in illicit activities, but they had failed to prove it in the previous case. With its opening, the Balinese Room came on the state government's radar. However, aside from its reputation for providing top entertainment, the Balinese Room was also known among state and local law enforcement officials for having an impenetrable entrance. This made making a new case against the Maceos surprisingly difficult.

As the Texas Rangers reported, the Maceos' used the architecture of the establishment to their advantage. The Balinese Room was built at the end of a pier that stretched many feet out from the coast. Toward the middle of the twentieth century, the Texas Rangers and other state enforcement officials attempted to arrest the Maceo brothers and their gamblers. However, the club's design allowed savvy workers to hide any trace of illegal activities prior to the officials' arrival in the gambling hall. Texas Ranger Ed Gooding explained, the "entrance was through doors fitted with electric locks at the sea wall. A lady was stationed in a booth at the entrance, and she would be smiling very sweetly. All the while, she was standing on a buzzer, warning the occupants that the Rangers were on their way."[264] This system allowed employees to quickly hide the gambling paraphernalia and any other evidence of foul play. All that was left in view were games such as "dominoes, pool, bridge, or checkers" and staff and customers "acting as innocent as newborn babies."[265]

The long hall that led to the gambling room at the Balinese Room became known as Rangers' Run. After being greeted by the smiling female at the door, the Texas Rangers would race down the long pier. As they progressed down Rangers' Run, "the band struck up 'The Eyes of Texas,' and the band leader announced, "And now, ladies and gentlemen, we give you, in person, the Texas Rangers!"[266] It was precautions and actions such as these that ensured that when raids did occur, they would be unsuccessful.

Decades after the Balinese Room had been shut down, journalist Cheryl Coggins Frink interviewed Adolfo Zamora and Buddy Kirk about their time spent working at the club. Zamora served as a chef in the 1950s, and Kirk was employed as the bandleader for several years. Zamora claimed that it took a little more than thirty seconds to clear the gambling equipment. He stated that "they had the gambling tables, but when they heard the Rangers, they used to press the button, and it [the table] turns around the other way and it was a setup like they were going to have a party of 8 or 10."[267]

The Maceo brothers were notorious for evading the investigations of state and local law enforcement agencies. In addition to the elaborate alarm system in place at the Balinese Room, the brothers had similar systems in some of their other gambling establishments. For example, one patron

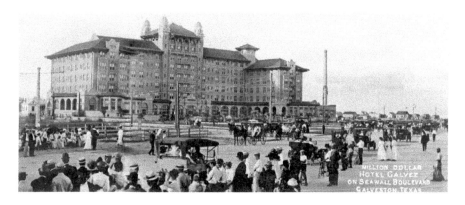

In addition to many entertainers who stayed at the Galvez Hotel, the Texas Rangers also occupied rooms there while investigating the Balinese Room. *Courtesy of the Library of Congress.*

recalled having to ring a doorbell at a nightclub known as Omar Khayyam. The patron explained that the doorbell was located within the bellybutton of a belly dancer painted on the front door of the establishment. Once the doorbell was rung, the belly dancer's eyes would open up so the doorman could ensure the visitor was not a local law enforcement officer or Texas Ranger attempting to enter the club.[268]

In addition to the drills and devices employed at their clubs, the Balinese Room had another alert system. As mentioned before, various city officials were reportedly corrupt. For example, police commissioner Walter L. Johnston was quoted as stating that he was on the payroll of forty-six whorehouses in the city of Galveston.[269] Although there are no official records of any officials being on the payroll of the Maceo family, there were unofficial claims of it. For example, crooked judges supposedly interfered with the Texas Rangers' investigations. One judge in particular would issue a search warrant and then immediately telephone the individuals targeted by the warrant. He would reportedly make a call and simply say, "Storm raising," and then quickly hang up.[270]

To supplement the help received from the local courts, the Maceo brothers had several other advocates working elsewhere within the local government. William J. Burns worked as a police officer early in his career, patrolling the red-light district. He was later promoted to Galveston's chief of police. His brother-in-law was Frank L. Biaggne, who served as the county sheriff. Ironically, both men served in their positions from 1933 to 1957—the years in which Galveston popularly operated as an open city.[271]

While serving as an elected official, Biaggne openly campaigned for an open city.[272] It is also rumored that he frequented the various gambling locations, not as a county official, but as a customer. This is a strong statement of the overwhelming tolerance seen among Galvestonians. Overall, Biaggne's reluctance to enforce the state's laws against gambling was not opposed by the majority of local voters. He was elected as sheriff for six different four-year terms. Interestingly, it was the same year that Biaggne was voted out of his position as sheriff and Burns ceased to serve as the island city's chief of police that the Maceos' empire finally crumbled. When asked later why he had never raided the Balinese Room, Biaggne simply stated that "the Balinese Room was a private club, he was not a member, and they would not let him in!"[273]

Each of the aforementioned provisions helped isolate Galveston's crime syndicate from outside law enforcement agencies' interference. However, as previously stated, there was a small movement against the island city's vice operations. Conservative religious members led the first movement. Then, as a result of the narcotics case against Sam Maceo, the Maceo brothers attracted greater attention from state agencies, putting them on the radar for the Texas Rangers through the 1940s and 1950s. Despite this increased official attention on the brothers' activities, it took almost two more decades for a successful indictment to be filed against the Maceos' empire, and this occurred only after both Sam and Rose were dead.

6

END OF AN ERA

DEATH OF THE MACEOS AND DEMISE OF THEIR EMPIRE

In the years following the dismissal of the narcotics case against Sam Maceo, the world of gambling witnessed a major change. Whereas Galveston had been operating various gambling establishments illegally for years, gambling was made legal in the state of Nevada in 1931. This provided a new legal venue with which various organized crime families would yearn to become involved. Crime syndicates from other large American cities operated businesses similar to those of the Maceo brothers. Unlike the Maceos, these other groups often did not operate in such tolerant locations, which created greater pressure to find more welcome venues. The change in Nevada's laws provided an attractive new opportunity for those groups operating outside the Free State of Galveston, but Maceo family members soon followed.

Prior to this enactment, the state of Nevada provided very little to the public. As historian Thomas Reppetto has written, "After its silver mines played out early in the century, it became a rest stop for cross-country travelers in the automobile era." Therefore, in order to boost its economy, the state legalized gambling. The following decade, there was a westward movement of crime syndicates investing in the legalized industry. For example, Bugsy Siegel opened the Flamingo at Las Vegas in 1946. Meyer Lansky and Moe Dalitz followed Siegel's move soon after.[274]

Overall, the emergence of legalized gambling had an effect on cities like Galveston. Galveston relied heavily on the economic support that derived from the Maceos' various gambling establishments. As previously discussed, places like the infamous Balinese Room attracted many tourists, some of whom were very affluent. Obviously visitors had to have a place to stay and a place to eat while on the island. Therefore, the clubs' visitors boosted the profits at local hotels and restaurants as well.

Unfortunately for Galveston, once gambling became legal elsewhere, people began to weigh the obvious consequences—a cost-benefit analysis. For workers and guests alike, there was a risk of being caught in the Maceos' entertainment venues. So why continue gambling in a city where it is illegal, when there is a city where it *is* legal? This simple realization naturally led to the movement west. The Maceos also recognized such an obvious idea. Sam acknowledged the same opportunities presented in Nevada that many other individuals had taken advantage of. However, in such a quickly changing environment, people were scrambling to get their hands on Las Vegas's earnings.

CHANGING TIMES: A WESTWARD MIGRATION

As previously mentioned, Al Capone became interested in Galveston's activities in the 1920s. It is likely he was not the only mob boss to see the potential for clubs like those made infamous on the island. Galveston's clubs had been the first of their kind. Unlike anything before, the island city's clubs offered top-ranked entertainment, the finest foods, gambling and alcohol—all under one roof. When crime groups saw the potential of Las Vegas, they opened establishments that mirrored those that had been run by the Maceos in Galveston for years.

While the rest of the country was experiencing these significant changes, Galveston was going through its own transitional period. After the narcotics case against Sam Maceo ended in 1942, the Maceos built an even greater reputation for themselves than ever before. As described, the opening of the Balinese Room marked a new epoch for the two brothers. However, they were already under the state government's microscope, and the new club brought increased publicity. Also because of the legalization of gambling in Nevada, the Maceos watched as many of their clients traveled west. Sam soon recognized the growing pressure on his operation in Galveston. Perhaps that is why he also tried to become involved in the movement west.

Sam used a previously valuable relationship to enter the Nevada market. Throughout Prohibition, Sam and Rose Maceo had developed an important relationship with Moe Dalitz. In the 1920s and 1930s, Dalitz led a Jewish crime syndicate in Cleveland, Ohio. Even during the early 1950s, after

Dalitz had moved west, Senator Estes Kefauver's Special Committee to Investigate Organized Crime listed him as one of the principal members of the Cleveland syndicate.[275] More importantly, throughout Prohibition, Dalitz and his crime family smuggled illegal liquors in from Canada, across Lake Erie. Unfortunately, Canadian authorities interrupted the group's bootlegging business.[276] Therefore, Dalitz formed a partnership with the Maceo brothers down in Galveston.

The liquor shipments received on the coast of Galveston were distributed to areas ranging from Detroit to Denver. Cleveland also became one of the inland locations to which the Maceo brothers shipped their smuggled alcohol. Shipments of liquor from Canada, originally sent across the Great Lakes and into Cleveland, were rerouted to Galveston. Then the liquor went north by railroad to Cleveland. One shipment confiscated by federal authorities consisted of over seven hundred cases of whiskey.[277] However, this bootlegging partnership was only the beginning of the Maceos' relationship with Dalitz.

In 1947, years after the end of Prohibition, Wilbur Clark provided the money to open a new hotel on the Las Vegas strip, the Desert Inn. Unfortunately, he was $90,000 short. For the next two years, the skeletal structure of the new hotel sat untouched. However, in 1949, Dalitz made a deal with Clark. Exactly what that deal was is not clear—different sources report different numbers. For example, journalist Gus Russo, an expert on organized crime, has reported that the Cleveland mob boss supplied Clark with the $90,000 that was needed for the hotel's construction, plus an additional $3.4 million to obtain a 74 percent ownership.[278] Yet historian Hal Rothman claimed that Dalitz put up a total of $1.3 million and took a 75 percent ownership.[279] Finally, Kefauver's United States Senate committee reported that Dalitz gave $1 million. This particular report claims the money was used to pay the necessary $90,000 for construction, as well as to purchase a 59 percent ownership.[280]

Although it is not clear how much money Dalitz put into the Desert Inn, it is obvious that he was involved in the establishment of the hotel. Clark would provide a front by operating the Desert Inn, while Dalitz would run the casinos. Soon after completing the construction, the partnership ran into a new problem. Due to a report released by the Chicago Crime Commission, Nevada authorities were reluctant to provide Dalitz with the required license to run the casino. Under Nevada law, anybody involved in gambling operations in Las Vegas was required to be licensed by the state, which meant obtaining a license through the Nevada State Tax Commission.

However, due to the Chicago Crime Commission's reports that Dalitz was directly involved in the Cleveland crime syndicate, the Nevada State Tax Commission was unwilling to release the necessary licensure.[281]

Undaunted, Dalitz contacted his old friend Sam Maceo. Dalitz was aware of Maceo's public relations. Particularly, he knew that Sam had built a good relationship with one of the United States senators from Nevada, Patrick McCarran. Apparently, at Dalitz's request, Sam met with McCarran at the senator's favorite spot, the Riverside Hotel in Reno.[282] It is unclear what occurred between the two gentlemen at the Riverside. Some speculate that Maceo simply paid McCarran. Nevertheless, obtaining the necessary license for Dalitz from the Nevada State Tax Commission was no longer an obstacle. The commission promptly issued what he needed in order to run the Desert Inn casino.[283]

When the Desert Inn opened in 1949, the Maceo brothers were among a list of guests who were allotted a certain amount of money in chips for gambling purposes. They were also the most pampered guests at the party.[284] After initially getting involved with the Desert Inn, Sam Maceo was interested in further establishing his mark in Las Vegas. As mentioned, the legalization of gambling there had prompted a migration west. Therefore, the Maceo brothers recognized the need to change with the times. Unfortunately, before they could transition to Las Vegas, the Maceo family crime syndicate experienced its greatest challenges yet.

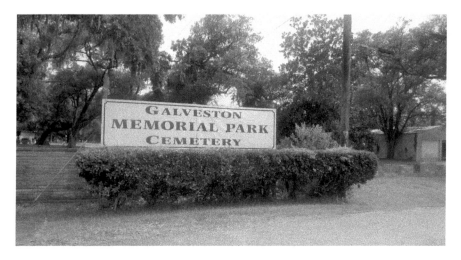

Both Sam and Rosario Maceo were buried in the Galveston Memorial Park Cemetery after passing away in the early 1950s. *Courtesy of Amanda Belshaw.*

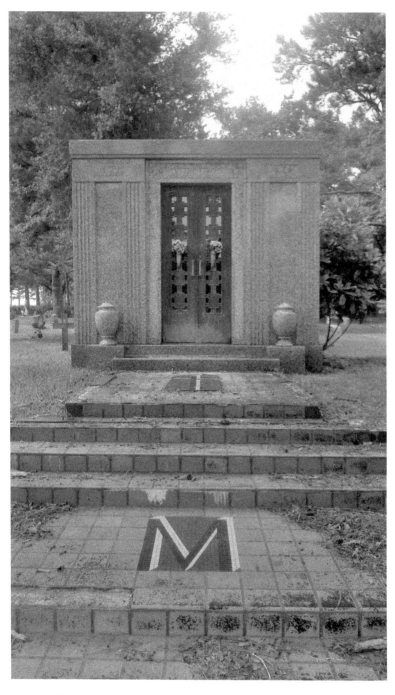

Rosario Maceo passed away shortly after his brother. Rosario was entombed in the Maceo mausoleum, while Sam is located directly outside. *Courtesy of Amanda Belshaw.*

On April 16, 1951, Sam Maceo passed away at John Hopkins Hospital in Baltimore, Maryland.[285] He had been suffering from cancer of the digestive tract. On March 28, he had undergone an operation, but unfortunately for him, he never made it out of the hospital. Funeral services were held on the following Thursday, after the family was able to transport the body back to Galveston.[286] Just months after Sam's death, it was reported that Rose Maceo was suffering from his own health problems.[287] Just a few years after Sam died, on March 15, 1954, Rose passed away from heart failure in his Galveston home.[288]

STATE INVESTIGATIONS: CLOSING THE DOORS OF AN ICONIC ESTABLISHMENT

While the Maceo family mourned the loss of its two leaders, a new set of indictments were handed down by the state courts against those involved in illicit activities in Galveston. Throughout the decade after Sam Maceo's extended narcotics conspiracy case, there were no serious investigations against the brothers' activities. Therefore, their illicit activities in the island city continued essentially uninterrupted until after Attorney General Price Daniel was elected in 1947. It appears that Daniel's motivation was not necessarily for the good of the community but was in fact a strategy linked to his ambitions for political advancement (he would become governor of Texas and a United States senator).

In general, the investigations that ensued almost a decade after Sam Maceo's narcotics trial resulted from a political movement against organized crime. Perhaps other candidates recognized that Governor James V. Allred had gained political support in the 1930s when he responded to local correspondence regarding the state's problem with organized crime. When Allred was governor, only a small majority, mostly religious conservatives, seemed to oppose the Galveston rackets. However, since then, Texas had seen a widespread change in attitude. Most cities' rackets had already been shut down. As a result, politicians recognized the potential political momentum that could be gained by cleaning up the remaining cities notorious for organized crime and rackets.

While Daniel proved to be the state official who finally had enough determination to bring down the Maceo organization, the operation was already beginning to crumble. The deaths of the brothers left their operation without proper leadership. Sam and Rosario had gained widespread support, not just for their activities, but also for how they operated their businesses on the island. Aside from his position at the top of Galveston's crime syndicate, Sam was well known for his charitable activism in the community. He supported such agencies as the Community Chest, Red Cross and American Cancer Fund.[289] Furthermore, because of Rose's Night Riders, "nobody locked their doors at night and no one was afraid to walk the streets at night."[290]

By the time Daniel and his successors targeted Galveston, Sam Maceo was already sick. Before the courts handed down any indictments, he passed away. Although Sam faced new charges in yet another narcotics case, he made it through his life without any convictions, despite his various rackets. Rosario, on the other hand, was still alive when Galveston was investigated. He was even named in a list of indictments in 1951. However, he, too, made it through his life without any convictions. Although on the radar of many state officials and agencies, the brothers appear to have been untouchable. But their passing left their organization exposed and weak, without the strong local support necessary to survive a legal assault by state law enforcement officials.

As mentioned, the investigations that occurred in the 1950s were the result of a political strategy. When Attorney General Daniel was elected to office, he had the intention of moving into the governor's seat. He used his position as attorney general as a steppingstone for his governorship. Like others after him, Daniel needed a way to attract some publicity for himself as a candidate for governor. Therefore, he became involved in the cleanup of organized crime. As journalist Robert Nieman has written, Daniel "became chair of the so-called 'little Kefauver hearings.'"[291] Galveston was believed to be the only city in the state of Texas to still allow bookmaking and gambling establishments to operate openly, so it attracted his attention.[292]

In 1951, Daniel worked toward shutting down the Maceo family's establishments, once and for all. It looked like he would be successful. In June, less than two months after Sam Maceo died, a Galveston newspaper reported that the attorney general had effectively shut down horse-race betting on the island. Daniel obtained an injunction "forbidding the Southwestern Bell Telephone Co. to permit use of its lines for transmission of race information to the Turf Athletic Club…and four other county spots."[293] Aside from the Turf Athletic Club, the establishments targeted in the suit included Murdoch's Pier, Home Plate Cigar Stand, the Chili Bowl in Kemah and the Streamline Dinner Club near Algoa.[294]

The suit provided details concerning the importance of the telephone lines and how exactly the Maceo family successfully relayed information across vast distances. Overall, the long-distance calls were costing the Maceos at least $1,000 each month.[295] It was suggested that these expensive telephone lines were being used to relay gambling information to bookies throughout Galveston County. The five establishments previously mentioned were well-known locations used for transmitting gambling information.

In addition to detailing the uses of the telephone lines, Daniel's suit named several members of the Maceo family crime syndicate. The suit named Maceo and Company, Rosario Maceo, Frank Maceo, Victor C. Maceo, Victor A. Maceo, Vincent A. Maceo, Joe T. Maceo, Sam T. Maceo, Anthony J. Fertitta, Victor J. Fertitta, Frank J. Fertitta, Sam Serio, A.J. Adams, O.E. Voight, Lorenzo Grillette, John B. Arena, Robert L. Fabj and Joe Salvato. It was estimated that the previous year's annual gross income from the gambling operation had totaled $349,267.94, which was plenty of money to attract the attention of such a long list of suspects.[296]

Overall, twenty-three indictments were handed down for Maceo family members and key players in their syndicate. However, each one slowly fell through the cracks in the Texas legal system. According to Nieman, after one year and five continuances, ten indictments were dismissed. Judge Charles Dibrell threw out the remaining thirteen indictments. Nieman also pointed out that Judge Dibrell was the father of Louis J. Dibrell, the attorney who had represented Sam Maceo throughout the New York narcotics case.[297] Perhaps these two men were also on the Maceos' payroll or supporters of maintaining an open city.

THE END OF AN ERA: CLOSING DOWN GALVESTON

Whether or not Charles and Louis Dibrell were on the Maceo family's payroll, they could not save the syndicate from the criminal charges filed by the state in 1957. Again, in a political move for the governor's seat, Galveston's illicit activities were under scrutiny. This time, it was Attorney General Will R. Wilson looking to finally bring an end to the island city's gambling. Wilson had new circumstances working in his favor. Both Sam and Rose Maceo had passed away by the time he began his extensive investigations. Since the two brothers' deaths, the Maceo family's operations had already begun to experience a change—a decline in support from locals.

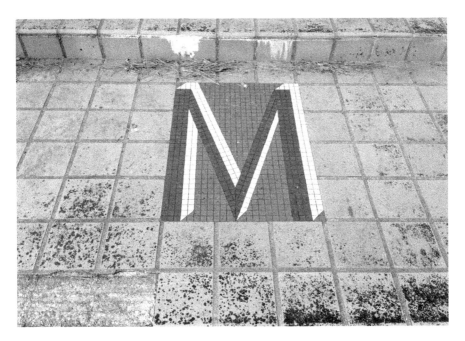

Both Sam and Rosario are buried within the Galveston Memorial Park Cemetery. *Courtesy of Amanda Belshaw.*

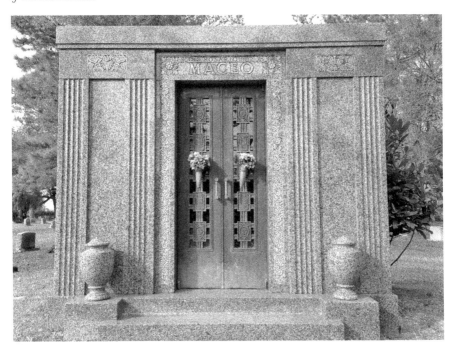

Rosario Maceo passed away on March 15, 1954, just a few years after Sam. Upon passing, his family entombed Rosario in the Maceo mausoleum. *Courtesy of Amanda Belshaw.*

This decline was attributed to various factors. As mentioned, a migration west had begun at the end of the 1940s. By 1957, there was an even stronger push toward expanding the new Las Vegas venue. More organized crime groups had sent people to the strip to collect at the gambling casinos. United States senator Estes Kefauver continued to use the famous Kefauver Committee as part of his political strategy to advance to the White House. His committee investigated organized crime across the country. Upon arriving in Las Vegas, federal investigators found that mobsters had fully infiltrated the city, despite the State of Nevada's attempt at regulation.

In addition to the movement west, Galvestonians were not as willing to support the illicit activities that occurred on their island without Sam and Rose Maceo at the head of the group. Sam had built up a reputation since the 1920s. As emphasized, he had an amiable character. Many residents believed that Sam was devoted to the well-being of Galveston and had their best interests in mind. Although Rose served in a more intimidating role, he, too, was well liked. Because of Rose and his Night Riders, the island city's residents had felt safe for years. Without the brothers at the head of Maceo family operations to draw popular support, the syndicate was beginning to crumble.

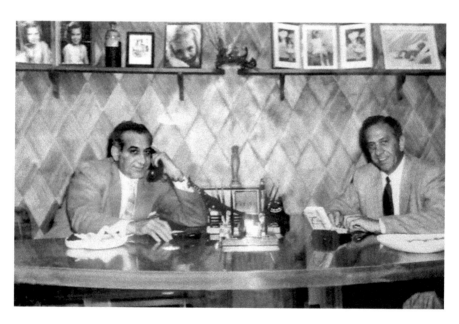

Located at Vic and Anthony's Steakhouse in Las Vegas is a picture of Victor and Anthony Fertitta hanging out in the infamous Balinese Room. *Courtesy of Amanda Belshaw via Vic and Anthony's Steakhouse.*

Before the Maceo brothers died, local historian Jean M. Brown claims the two were "grooming" their nephews Anthony J. and Victor J. Fertitta to continue operating their establishments.[298] These two were the sons of Joseph Frances "Frank" Fertitta and Olivia Maceo Fertitta, older sister of Sam and Rose. However, Anthony and Victor seemed to lack a suave character like that of Sam. The Fertittas proved to be not nearly as popular on the island. Nieman attributes their failed attempt to the migration west.[299] However, Brown attributes it to the changing environment in Galveston at the end of World War II. The returning veterans had new ideas about the future of their island city, and these did not include tolerance for organized crime.[300]

Perhaps their failed attempt at keeping the open city alive was due to multiple factors—maybe Nieman *and* Brown were correct. It is also very likely that the Fertitta brothers did not have complementary personalities like those of Sam and Rose. Sam was the gracious, amiable frontman, while Rose kept everyone in line. Although Rose played a vital role, he usually remained in the shadows of the operations, and his enforcement efforts did not generate a lot of negative publicity. Unlike the Maceos, it was not long before the Fertittas had attracted negative attention from the news media, which would have alienated veterans looking for a better image for their community.

After the passing of Sam and Rose Maceo, their nephews Anthony and Victor became "the owners of several plush gambling clubs in Galveston and [controlled] several others."[301] Despite the passing of the senior Maceos, Galveston still retained a reputation for being a "wide-open city." According to one magazine company, the illicit activities on the island had outlived those in other Texas cities; it was called "the last sin city."[302] Therefore, *Time* magazine sent a couple of photographers to Galveston to capture the current state of affairs. The two men assigned to the project were Henry Suydam and Joe Scherschel.

While on assignment, the two men were seen photographing the Turf Athletic Club. When Anthony Fertitta was notified, he, along with a few associates, chased the photographers back to the Galvez Hotel, where Fertitta hit Suydam in the face.[303] The incident earned the Fertittas significant attention, mainly from non-Galvestonians. *Time* magazine ran the article, as intended. Two pages of photos were published, revealing prostitution houses still in operation, as well as gambling locations. The article even provided a picture of Suydam's face after being hit by Fertitta at the Galvez Hotel.[304]

Although the *Time* article offered more pictures than words, the magazine brought national attention to the illicit activities that were still occurring in Galveston. It can be argued that this is what brought the next round of investigations from the state. Popular opinion remains that Wilson acted in his own best interest when he began his case against Galveston. However, others believe that the shaken photographer and the published article provoked Wilson. With national attention on the island city's activities, he was left with no choice but to act to prevent further negative publicity. What is certain is that the senior Maceo brothers would never have been so careless as to antagonize the media, nor would they have provided such an easy opportunity for a state law enforcement official to capitalize on negative publicity about them.

The Maceos' nephews also made other key mistakes. Without Sam and Rose Maceo around to oppose the idea, the clubs started skimming for extra profit. The new leaders of the family syndicate also failed to keep city officials on payroll, as Sam and Rose had done over the years. As Nieman states, "In the past, the police, judges, and others in power never had to shake down the club owners for protection because Sam and Rose had made sure that those in control were always taken care of. Not now. Sheriff [Frank L.] Biaggne went around to the clubs and demanded money if the owners wanted to stay in business." Nieman adds, "Desperately trying to stem the tide running against them, the owners went to their business friends, who had been profiting for decades because of them, and asked for their help. The businessmen dutifully went to Attorney General Will Wilson and asked him to rein in Sheriff Biaggne."[305]

Instead of reining in Sheriff Biaggne as requested of him, Wilson took the chance to shut down Galveston's rackets and secure some votes for his own race for governor. After several failed attempts at shutting down the gambling establishments in Galveston, the attorney general and Texas Rangers had to get creative. They had learned that no matter how secretive they were, raids would fail in Galveston. This was due to the lingering popularity of the illicit activities and the various city officials and judges who remained on the syndicates' payroll, now run by the Fertitta brothers. Therefore, the rangers began to sit in various club locations night after night.[306]

Under the guidance of Captain John J. Klevenhagen, the Texas Rangers entered the Galveston clubs each night upon opening, bearing guns and wearing their infamous ranger hats. As a result of their continued presence, the Maceo family removed the gambling paraphernalia from their clubs. At the same time, because of the rangers' presence, the clubs' overall business declined. Regular customers were made nervous by the observant rangers.[307]

After pursuing the illegal operators for an extended time, the Texas Rangers finally discovered a small portion of the island's gambling

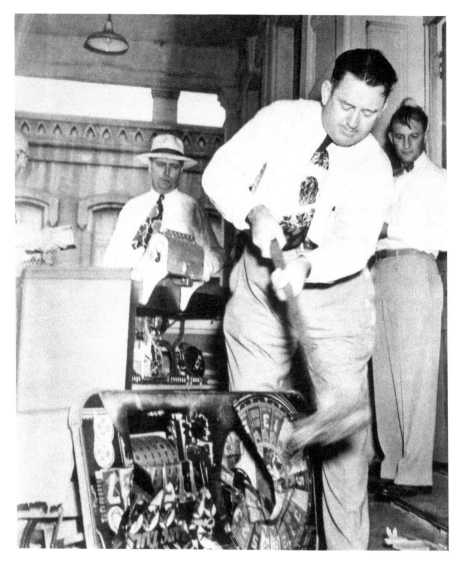

After locating about $2 million worth of gambling paraphernalia, the Texas Rangers smashed and disposed of the equipment for a publicity stunt. *Courtesy of the Rosenberg Library.*

paraphernalia. On June 19, 1957, the rangers "confiscated more than 50 gambling machines and more than 200 cases of Up books."[308] According to ranger Ed Gooding, the collection of illicit paraphernalia totaled about $800,000, but the rangers knew they still had not found the main stash of equipment.[309]

Gooding later recalled that he was working with another ranger, Pete Rogers, when two of the state's investigating agents approached them hastily and declared they had found what was referred to as the mother lode. The majority of the Maceo family's collection of gambling equipment had been stashed away in the Hollywood Dinner Club, which had been shut down for years. The most recently discovered equipment had a total value of $1.2 million. It included "1,500 slot machines, roulette wheels, blackjack tables, dice tables, and box after box of chips and dice."[310]

The discovery of this tremendous cache caused a huge financial loss for the Balinese Room. However, the Fertitta brothers tried to hang on to their business. Almost a year later to the day, the Balinese Room managed to sell all of its tickets for a show by "Chico the Laughing Cuban" and his orchestra. The "new" club featured legitimate billiards when the doors reopened, as well as bridge tables for card games.[311] Despite their efforts, under the close watch of the Texas Rangers, the club never prospered like it had prior to the raids that shut down the gambling. Ultimately, the collection of $2 million worth of gambling equipment led to the final closing of the Balinese Room.

After the success of the Texas Rangers, the new Maceo family syndicate leaders and their associates faced a long list of indictments. According to the *Galveston Daily News*, a grand jury returned a record number of indictments, the majority of which were for gaming violations. Both Anthony and Victor Fertitta faced five indictments for their involvement in illegal gaming. The indictments handed down to dozens of defendants included "keeping a gambling house, keeping and exhibiting a slot machine, possession of a slot machine, and permitting premises to be used for gambling."[312] After multiple continuances and various delays, Anthony Fertitta was found guilty on only one count and received a two-year suspended sentence.[313] The local newspapers never reported the outcome of Victor Fertitta's indictments. However, considering the outcome of his brother's case, it is likely he was not found guilty on any of the major charges.

CONTINUING THE MACEO BROTHERS' LEGACY

As previously described, when Sam and Rose Maceo passed away in the early 1950s, their nephews Anthony J. and Victor J. Fertitta took over the family business. Before dying, the Maceo brothers had begun preparing Anthony

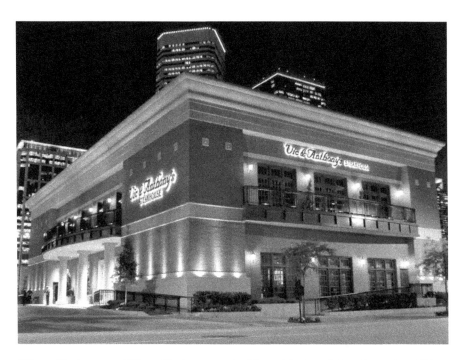

Tillman Fertitta, son of Victor Fertitta, opened a Vic and Anthony's Steakhouse in addition to several other restaurant chains. *Courtesy of www.downtownhouston.org*

and Victor to take over their various establishments.[314] Unfortunately, as illustrated, the Fertittas did not meet with the acceptance and success enjoyed by their predecessors. It was not long before Attorney General Wilson and the Texas Rangers stormed the island and closed down their gambling establishments.

After Wilson's team smashed up the confiscated gambling paraphernalia, over one hundred indictments were handed down to numerous club owners and their business associates. As already noted, Victor and Anthony Fertitta were among those who were handed indictments. However, a third Fertitta brother, Frank J. Fertitta, was not indicted for any crimes in Galveston.[315] And his son, Frank J. Fertitta Jr., proved to be perhaps the most capable of the heirs of Sam and Rose Maceo. After Galveston's underworld was shut down, the younger Frank continued the Maceos' legacy in Las Vegas, as Sam and Rose had intended to do.

When Frank arrived in Las Vegas with his wife and first child, he started as a card dealer. He first worked as a 21 dealer at the Stardust Casino. During his early years, he progressed quickly from a card dealer to a floor man at the

Tropicana Club, to a shift manager and a "baccarat manager"" at Circus Circus and, finally, to a general manager at the Fremont Casino. According to historian Alan R. Balboni, during this time, Frank began to consider owning his own gambling establishment. Therefore, he partnered with an associate, Carl Thomas, and went to see some Valley Bank executives. Valley Bank reportedly had worked with the Teamsters Union, which partnered with various mob members to continue adding to the burgeoning strip. With a loan from Valley Bank, Fertitta and Thomas opened the Bingo Palace not far from the main Las Vegas strip in 1977.[316]

Then, in 1983, Fertitta's partner, Thomas, was indicted along with several others in a federal case against casino operator Frank L. Rosenthal and his associates. Thomas had been recorded on a federal wiretap explaining the process of skimming the casinos in Las Vegas. Thomas explained how the Vegas mobsters had taken $2 million from casinos.[317] As soon as Thomas's legal troubles began, Fertitta bought all of his partner's shares in the Bingo Palace, as well as a third partner's shares.[318]

Despite his efforts to separate himself from the legal troubles, investigators remained interested in Fertitta. Their reasoning was that he had been employed at three clubs found to be participating in the skimming; therefore, he must have been involved. Then, during what was referred to as the "Stardust Skimming Trial," a witness stated that a man named Frank had in fact been involved in the skimming at his casino. The investigations against Frank Fertitta continued for four years. In the end, all charges were dropped against the Maceo heir apparent due to a lack of evidence.[319]

Despite the ongoing allegations against him, Fertitta used his network of Las Vegas connections to continue the expansion of his own empire. It is likely that he considered the lessons he had learned from his great-uncles Sam and Rose Maceo while working in Galveston. He began mirroring Sam's earlier efforts to gain public support. According to Balboni, Frank donated $300,000 to the University of Nevada–Las Vegas. The next year, he contributed another $1 million to the same university's tennis complex. Around the same time, he also donated $70,000 to Leslie Randolph, who had accumulated a significant amount of debt in medical bills due to her daughter's need for a heart transplant.[320]

After overcoming the accusations against him in the 1980s, Fertitta further expanded his businesses. The Bingo Palace became known as the Palace Station. By 1993, Fertitta had managed to go public with Station Casinos, a company that had developed from his early Palace Station.[321] His sons, Lorenzo and Frank J. Fertitta III, quickly built an even greater empire out

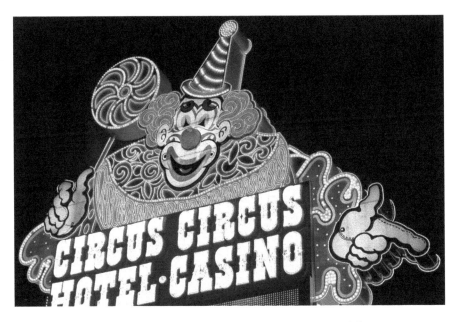

Circus Circus Casino sign in Las Vegas, Nevada. *Courtesy of the Library of Congress.*

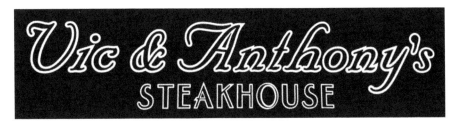

In addition to the Houston location of Vic and Anthony's Steakhouse, Tillman Fertitta also established locations in Las Vegas and Atlantic City. *Courtesy of Amanda Belshaw.*

of the family business as young adults. They continued the Maceo family legacy, which began in Galveston, with Station Casinos. In addition, to continuing to operate Station Casinos, in 2001, the Fertitta brothers invested in the Ultimate Fighting Championship.[322]

Although the Maceo brothers and their operations did not survive the 1950s, their influence lasted through the end of the century. Frank J. Fertitta Jr., their great-nephew, carried on their legacy many states away in Las Vegas. Fertitta learned many valuable lessons as a young man from the Maceos. Perhaps he learned more than his two uncles, Anthony J. and

Victor J. Fertitta, who had been brought down with the rest of the island city's rackets. Despite the legal troubles he faced in Nevada, Frank proved that he understood how to run a lucrative business that his sons could also operate with great success. Even today, Sam and Rose's descendants are doing the same thing in Las Vegas that they were doing almost a century ago in Galveston.

7

LEGACY OF THE MACEOS

G alveston was not the only American city with gambling, prostitution and alcohol. Nor was it the only city in Texas that offered illegal forms of entertainment. However, Galveston earned much more attention than its rivals at the peak of the Maceo family's island empire during the twentieth century. The famous Kefauver Committee hardly recognized other locations in Texas. Beyond the group's investigations in places like Missouri and Ohio, the congressmen were interested in Sam Maceo and his associate Biaggio Angelica, who resided in nearby Houston.[323]

Galveston maintained its reputation as an open city through the first half of the twentieth century. This remains the most significant fact about the vice activities in Galveston—about the legacy of the Maceos. As one article in the *Galveston Daily News* stated, "These activities had been prevalent all over Texas from the earliest days. Galveston just did not go along with the new morality when the rest of the state did. Activities that were commonplace everywhere at one time continued to be commonplace here after they had ceased or gone underground in the rest of Texas."[324]

Without the efforts from state agencies like the attorney general's team and the Texas Rangers, Galveston would probably have retained its illegal entertainment venues much longer. Although the Maceos had experienced some small opposition, they were still widely popular. Left to the local law enforcement agencies, the Maceos and their descendants would not have been faced with legal ramifications. Ultimately, such ramifications finally reduced the island's illicit activities.

As pointed out, there were various historical factors that created a suitable environment for the Maceos' organized crime operations. Long before the Maceo brothers arrived on Galveston Island, illicit activities occurred. The various transient populations provided a tolerant environment for vices such as gambling, prostitution and the consumption of alcohol. In addition, the residents of Galveston endured several catastrophic events in their early history. After surviving these horrible events, the island failed to experience further growth. Instead, Galveston faced a noticeable economic decline. The various vice activities of Galveston remedied the island's recession.

In addition to the environmental factors on the island that cultivated criminal behavior, the Maceo brothers bore certain characteristics and knowledge that aided in their overall success. Because of their history in Sicily, Sam and Rose understood how organized crime groups operated. More importantly, they realized what behaviors and actions would win the public's support. Then, upon arriving in America, Sam gained firsthand experience about mob activities in southern Louisiana.

These environmental factors and cultural experiences became catalysts for the Maceos' involvement and success in Galveston. Within a relatively short period of time, Sam and Rose Maceo became deeply involved in the existing vice activities. Moreover, they soon took over the island's illicit activities. The brothers exploited the island city's geographic location, like those before them. Plus, they won the hearts of the community members through charitable contributions and by providing entertainment and security.

It appears the Maceos did more than simply place their city officials on the syndicate's payroll. The support of the two brothers extended well beyond financial compensations, although there are suggestions that payments were of course made. In addition, the brothers maintained widespread support within the community by putting the city's best interests first. That was the opinion of many residents—that the Maceo brothers, especially Sam, truly loved Galveston. Despite his less admirable criminal behavior, Sam continued to provide aid and funding to the island and its residents until his death in 1951.

Also important to consider is that aside from the extensive coverage the Maceos received for a few court cases, their activities seemed to have gone largely unnoticed by outsiders. Locals, of course, understood what was occurring in their backyards. Even non-Galvestonians knew that the island had a reputation for its illicit activities, yet there was little coverage in newspapers. The majority of public coverage occurred when Sam Maceo faced narcotics charges in the late 1930s and early 1940s. Then, in 1951,

Sam Maceo is Kindly King Of Texas Gambling Realm

Local and national coverage of the Maceos and their clubs. Court cases, grand openings and big entertainers were covered by newspapers. *Courtesy of Fredericksburg's Freelance-Star.*

various news sources reported when the courts handed down a large number of indictments. However, when the indictments were thrown out, the public seemed to lose interest in the fate of the Maceos.

Those who did disapprove of the Maceos' establishments and the activities that were hidden behind their elaborate alarm systems made up an insignificant minority. This small group voiced their concerns to state officials, hoping outside interference would shut down the Free State of Galveston. Yet the island's vices were insulated from those outside forces through various payoffs and local support. The island's residents provided a better alarm system than the systems installed at the doors of the clubs. The club owners and their customers felt little threat, knowing they would receive a phone call or hear idle talk from Galvestonians.

Considering the significant amount of literature covering Galveston's turbulent history, there is very little information written on the Maceo brothers. The two men had a significant influence in Galveston during the first half of the twentieth century. Even after their deaths, their legacy was kept alive. As discussed earlier, the two brothers' extended family carried on the family business. First, their nephews Anthony J. and Victor J. Fertitta attempted to continue the Maceo legacy in Galveston. Unfortunately for them, they were not very successful. However, the Fertittas' nephew Frank J. Fertitta Jr. (who would have been a great-nephew of Sam and Rose Maceo) enjoyed considerable success in Las Vegas.

Why would he not find such success? Frank essentially went to Las Vegas to continue what he was already good at doing. The lack of legal convictions against the family is a testament to how well they did their jobs, admirable or not. Las Vegas simply provided a larger playground. As mentioned, other crime families had shown interest in the Maceos' activities. When Las Vegas opened its doors to illicit activities, such organizations took advantage of the new opportunity, and the Maceo family followed suit. It is plausible that the Maceos inspired the lucrative businesses found on the Vegas strip

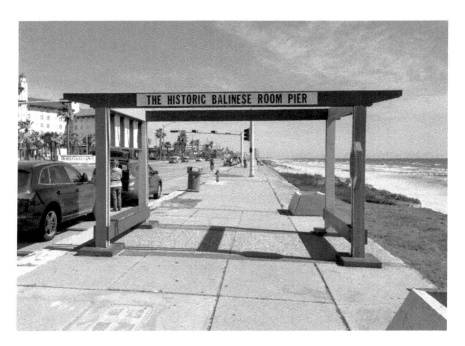

A small memorial on the Seawall is all that remains of the infamous Balinese Room after being destroyed by Hurricane Ike. *Courtesy of Amanda Belshaw.*

today—entertainment, gambling, alcohol and food, all under a single roof. Naturally, this was the best place for Frank to relocate.

Sadly, most of the tourists ebbing in and out of the Station Casinos are not aware of the rich history that provided Frank with the knowledge and experience to succeed in Nevada. They do not realize that what is now a Las Vegas legacy began several state lines away. Even more unfortunately, the tourists of Galveston have little to no knowledge of the considerable island history. Since the destruction of the Balinese Room in 2008, when the island was hit by a terrible hurricane, there is little physical evidence of Sam and Rose's activities—of their dozens of establishments and widespread illicit operations. The legacy of the Maceo family empire continues to fade with the memory of those who lived through some of Galveston's most exciting years.

NOTES

CHAPTER 1

1. Mallory, *Understanding Organized Crime*, 110–11.
2. Ibid., 19–20, 110.
3. Ibid., 19.
4. Marinbach, *Galveston*, xii–xv.
5. Burka, "Grande Dame."
6. McComb, *Galveston*, 42–44.
7. Bixel and Turner, *Galveston and the Storm*, 2.
8. Burka, "Grande Dame."
9. Barnstone, *Galveston That Was*, 13.
10. Hardwick, *Mythic Galveston*, 60–62.
11. Marinbach, *Galveston*, xii–xv.
12. Burka, "Grande Dame"; Bixel and Turner, *Galveston and the Storm*, 5–6.
13. Hardwick, *Mythic Galveston*, 28–59.
14. Ibid., 95–96.
15. McComb, *Galveston*, 93–97.
16. Remmers, *Portrait of Galveston Island*, 19; Bixel and Turner, *Galveston and the Storm*, 6–8.
17. Collins, *Tragedies*, 22.
18. Burka, "Grande Dame"; McComb, *Galveston*, 138–43. The elevation at the wall was increased a total of 18 feet. Moving farther inland, the grade was decreased 1 foot for every 1,500 feet.

19. McComb, *Galveston*, 48; Burka, "Grande Dame."

20. Nieman, "Galveston's Balinese Room," 8–9.

21. Remmers, *Going Down the Line*, 3.

22. The Volstead Act was also known as the National Prohibition Act and was in place from its enactment in 1919 until it was repealed in 1933. The intention of the Volstead Act was to prohibit the consumption, sale and transportation of alcoholic beverages throughout the United States.

23. Beales, *Risorgimento*, 13–39; Clark, *Italian Risorgimento*, 75–92.

24. Brown, *Free Rein*, 24–36.

25. Nieman, "Galveston's Balinese Room," 6–7.

26. Burka, "Grande Dame"; McComb, *Galveston*, 40–56; Cartwright, *Galveston*, 214–15.

CHAPTER 2

27. U.S. Bureau of the Census, "2010 Census Report."

28. U.S. Bureau of the Census, "American Community Survey."

29. Burka, "Grande Dame."

30. U.S. Bureau of the Census, "American Community Survey."

31. Marinbach, *Galveston*, xii–xv.

32. Remmers, *Going Down the Line*, 3–24.

33. Hardwick, *Mythic Galveston*, 1.

34. Remmers, *Portrait of Galveston Island*, 7–13, 19.

35. Collins, *Tragedies*, 22.

36. Cartwright, *Galveston*, 207–08; Remmers, *Going Down the Line*, 24.

37. Remmers, *Going Down the Line*, 24.

38. Burka, "Grande Dame."

39. Hayes, *Galveston*, 8.

40. Ibid., 9.

41. Carol A. Lipscomb, "Karankawa Indians," Handbook of Texas Online, uploaded June 15, 2010. Published by the Texas State Historical Association. http://www.tshaonline.org/handbook/online/articles/bmk05 (accessed April 20, 2014).

42. Cartwright, *Galveston*, 8–9, 18–19; Hayes, *Galveston*, 8–9; McComb, *Galveston*, 32–33. McComb presents both perspectives on the occurrence of cannibalism on Galveston Island. He leaves it to the reader to decide which group participated in cannibalism. When telling about the Spaniards consuming the flesh of their own men, he points out that these

men thus *involuntarily* stayed on the island for the next six years. He stated that in outrage against the Spaniards' actions, the Karankawas forced the remaining men "to work as medicine men and slaves."

43. Hayes, *Galveston*, 8–9.
44. Ibid., 34.
45. Hardwick, *Mystic Galveston*, 21–23.
46. McComb, *Galveston*, 35.
47. Ibid., 33–34.
48. Hardwick, *Mystic Galveston*, 22.
49. McComb, *Galveston*, 42–44.
50. Burka, "Grande Dame."
51. Barnstone, *Galveston That Was*, 19.
52. McComb, *Galveston*, 47, 151–59.
53. Hardwick, *Mystic Galveston*, 67–69.
54. Ibid., 69.
55. Young, *Galveston and the Great West*, 67–69.
56. McComb, *Galveston*, 4–6, 49–53.
57. Remmers, *Going Down the Line*, 5.
58. Ibid., 10.
59. Bixel and Turner, *Galveston and the Storm*, 2.
60. McComb, *Galveston*, 108–09; Remmers, *Going Down the Line*, 7.
61. Hardwick, *Mystic Galveston*, 3, 76; Remmers, *Portrait of Galveston*, 15.
62. Hardwick, *Mystic Galveston*, 76.
63. Blocker, Fahey and Tyrrell, *Alcohol and Temperance*, 323–25.
64. Remmers, *Portrait of Galveston*, 7–13.
65. McComb, *Galveston*, 93–97.
66. Hardwick, *Mystic Galveston*, 34, 72.
67. McComb, *Galveston*, 26–31; Hardwick, *Mystic Galveston*, 95–96.
68. McComb, *Galveston*, 26–31.
69. Burka, "Grande Dame."
70. Larson, *Isaac's Storm*, 83–84.
71. McComb, *Galveston*, 121–22; Young, *Galveston and the Great West*, 199; Collins, *Tragedies*, 35. McComb explains that there are many different estimates, some as high as ten to twelve thousand deaths. Young estimates about six thousand people falling victim to the storm. Collins states that although initial estimates were around six thousand, the final estimate was eight to ten thousand.
72. Green, *Story of the Hurricane*, 3–5.
73. Cartwright, *History of the Island*, 161.

74. Ibid., 118–19.
75. Cartwright, "One Last Shot."
76. Burka, "Grande Dame."
77. Barnstone, *Galveston That Was*, 27; McComb, *Galveston*, 47.
78. Barnstone, *Galveston That Was*, 15–18; McComb, *Galveston*, 48.
79. Barnstone, *Galveston That Was*, 15–18.
80. McComb, *Galveston*, 57–61.
81. Ibid., 138–43.
82. Ibid., 150.
83. Burka, "Grande Dame."
84. *Galveston Daily News*, "Galveston Surf Bathing Company," August 13, 1881, http://access.newspaperarchive.com/galveston-daily-news/1881-08-13 (accessed August 28, 2013).
85. McComb, *Galveston*, 64–65.
86. Cartwright, *Galveston*, 7.
87. Collins, *Tragedies*, 23–24.

CHAPTER 3

88. Mallory, *Understanding Organized Crime*, 110–11. Mallory argues that by the time Italy was unified in 1859, criminals had already developed into powerful and organized groups.
89. Beales, *Risorgimento*, 32–35.
90. Clark, *Italian Risorgimento*, 75.
91. Dickie, *Cosa Nostra*, 35.
92. Saladino, *Italy from Unification*, 79.
93. Reppetto, *American Mafia*, 6–7.
94. Mallory, *Understanding Organized Crime*, 111.
95. Reppetto, *American Mafia*, 7.
96. Saladino, *Italy from Unification*, 59. It is reported that conditions became so bad that the assets of about eighty-two thousand people were confiscated.
97. Repetto, *American Mafia*, 7.
98. U.S. Bureau of the Census, "Fifteenth Census, 1930," Texas, Galveston County; U.S. Customs Service, "Passenger Lists of Vessels."
99. Mallory, *Understanding Organized Crime*, 110.
100. Shanabruch, "Louisiana Immigration Movement," 204, 212–20.
101. Ibid., 221–23.
102. Reppetto, *American Mafia*, 7.

103. Brown, *Free Rein*, 24.

104. Reppetto, *American Mafia*, 7.

105. Mallory, *Understanding Organized Crime*, 19. Mallory also reports organized crime groups within Jewish and Irish communities throughout the major United States cities.

106. Scarpaci, "Immigrants in the New South," 166.

107. Saladino, *Italy from Unification*, 20. Brigand groups formed before the unification of Italy. They developed as a result of the lack of legitimate economic opportunities in Sicily and Naples.

108. Shanabruch, "Louisiana Immigration Movement," 223.

109. Dickie, *Cosa Nostra*, 217; Reppetto, *American Mafia*, 5–7.

110. Mallory, *Understanding Organized Crime*, 19.

111. U.S. Bureau of the Census, "Fifteenth Census, 1930," Texas, Galveston County.

112. U.S. Bureau of the Census, "Thirteenth Census, 1910," Louisiana, Leesville Ward 3. Various sources suggest Frank Maceo was involved in the illicit activities of his brothers, but there is no actual evidence. If he was indeed involved, he remained out of the public eye. Records also show that Vittorio and Angelina had another child, Gaetano, who was born in 1892 but only lived until 1897.

113. U.S. Bureau of the Census, "Fifteenth Census, 1930," Texas, Galveston County; U.S. Customs Service, "Passenger Lists of Vessels."

114. Brown, *Free Rein*, 24.

115. Reppetto, *American Mafia*, 8.

116. U.S. Department of War, "Draft Registration Cards."

117. Chalfant, *Galveston*, 16–19.

118. Mallory, *Understanding Organized Crime*, 112.

119. Remmers, *Going Down the Line*, 7–24.

120. Brown, *Free Rein*, 26–27.

121. Burka, "Grande Dame."

122. Cartwright, *Galveston*, 212–13.

123. Ibid., 212.

124. Ibid.

125. Brown, *Free Rein*, 25.

126. *Port Arthur News*, "Sam Maceo, Galveston Gambling Man, Weeps When Freed of Charges of Dope Peddling," October 25, 1942, http://access.newspaperarchive.com/port-arthur-news/1942-10-25/page-12 (accessed July 15, 2013).

127. Cartwright, *Galveston*, 212.

128. Brown, *Free Rein*, 34–35.
129. *Galveston Daily News*, "Ex-Barber Runs Plushy Game Room in Texas," April 23, 1947, http://access.newspaperarchive.com/galveston-daily-news/1947-10-03/ (accessed October 3, 2013).

CHAPTER 4

130. Remmers, *Going Down the Line*, 3.
131. Burka, "Grande Dame."
132. *Lubbock Morning Avalanche*, "Rum Runners Captured Off Galveston Coast," January 5, 1924, http://access.newspaperarchive.com/morning-avalanche/1924-01-05 (accessed October 4, 2013).
133. *Victoria Advocate*, "British Motorboat Forfeited by Order of Federal Judge," May 29, 1925, http://access.newspaperarchive.com/victoria-advocate/1925-05-29 (accessed October 3, 2013); *Galveston Daily News*, "Tomako Seized on Washington Orders," November 27, 1923, http://access.newspaperarchive.com/galveston-daily-news/1923-11-27 (accessed October 3, 2013).
134. *Galveston Daily News*, "Well-known Criminals Called Isle Home in '30s," December 11, 1996, http://access.newspaperarchive.com/galveston-daily-news/1996-12-11 (accessed December 5, 2013).
135. Cartwright, *Galveston*, 238–39.
136. Nieman, "Galveston's Balinese Room," 10.
137. *Fort Worth Star-Telegram*, "Find Body of Wife in Clump of Bushes," November 4, 1921, http://genealogybank.com/gbnk/newspapers/doc (accessed October 7, 2013).
138. *Orange Leader*, "Galveston Flier Found Dying on Beach Sidewalk," April 21, 1933, http://texashistory.unt.edu/ark:/67531/metapth289371/ (accessed September 12, 2013).
139. *Orange Leader*, "Slain Aviator Identified As Holdup Man," April 23, 1933, http://texashistory.unt.edu/ark:/67531/metapth289372 (accessed September 13, 2013).
140. *Galveston Daily News*, "Young Flyer Facing Trial in Kidnaping Assassinated: Charge of Murder Is Filed against Rose Maceo after Shooting Affray," April 21, 1933, http://access.newspaperarchive.com/Galveston-daily-news/1933-04-21 (accessed January 20, 2014).
141. Ibid.

142. *Galveston Daily News*, "Bond for Maceo Is Reduced at Hearing: Only One Witness Testifies at Preliminary Trial in Murder Case," April 30, 1933, http://access.newspaperarchive.com/galveston-daily-news/1933-04-30 (accessed December 21, 2013).

143. *Galveston Daily News*, "Maceo: Apparently No-Billed by Jury: Crawford Refuses to Comment but No Indictment Returned," May 27, 1933, http://access.newspaperarchive.com/galveston-daily-news/1933-05-27 (accessed December 21, 2013).

144. Nieman, "Galveston's Balinese Room," 6–10.

145. Brown, *Free Rein*, 28–29.

146. Ibid.

147. Humble, *Frank Nitti*.

148. Cartwright, *Galveston*, 210–11.

149. Ibid.

150. Brown, *Free Rein*, 45–46.

151. Ibid.

152. Ibid.

153. *Galveston Daily News*, "Two Galvestonians and Crew of British Schooner Face Charges: Complaints Are Filed; Zinn Indicates Cases of Men Closely Allied," January 9, 1924, http://access.newspaperarchive. com/galveston-daily-news/1924-01-09 (accessed October 4, 2013).

154. Ibid.

155. *Galveston Daily News*, "Conviction of Nounes and Varnell Affirmed by Federal High Court," March 12, 1925, http://access.newspaperarchive.com/galveston-daily-news/1925-03-12 (accessed November 13, 2013).

156. *Galveston Daily News*, "Injunction Issued Against Roseland: Attorney General's Department Alleges Gambling at Club There," August 18, 1927, http://access.newspaperarchive.com/galveston-daily-news/ 1927-08-18 (accessed November 15, 2013).

157. *Galveston Daily News*, "Liquor Conspiracy Charge Filed Here: Musey and Nounes Are Held Under $10,000 Bonds in Case," February 12, 1929, http://access.newspaperarchive.com/galveston-daily-news/1939-02-12 (accessed November 13, 2013).

158. *Galveston Daily News*, "Nounes and Musey in Jail Here to Await Sentence of Court," May 12, 1929, http://access.newspaperarchive.com/ galveston-daily-news/1929-05-12 (accessed November 13, 2013).

159. *Galveston Tribune*, "Musey Case on Federal Docket: Court Will Open Here Monday," February 22, 1930, http://access.newspaperarchive. com/galveston-tribune/1930-02-22 (accessed November 20, 2013).

160. McComb, *Galveston*, 160–61.

161. Ibid.

162. Brown, *Free Rein*, 27–46.

163. *Galveston Daily News*, "Gun Battle," March 15, 1931, http://access. newspaperarchive.com/galveston-daily-news/1931-03-15   (accessed January 20, 2014).

164. *Galveston Daily News*, "One Dead After Down-Town Gun Fight: Gregory Fatally Hits; Owens and Crabb Are Charged with Death," March 14, 1931, http://access.newspaperarchive.com/galveston-daily-news/1931-03-14 (accessed January 20, 2014).

165. *Galveston Daily News*, "Owens Appeal Motion to Be Heard Today," November 18, 1931, http://access/ newspaperarchive.com/galveston-daily-news/1931-11-18 (accessed January 21, 2014).

166. *Galveston Daily News*, "Frankovich Is Charged with Displaying Gun: Protection Asked of Police in Houston," http://access. newspaperarchive.com/galveston-daily-news/1931-03-24   (accessed March 24, 1931).

167. Chalfant, *Galveston*, 86.

168. Brown, *Free Rein*, 27–46.

169. Ibid., 34–35.

170. Nieman, "Galveston's Balinese Room."

171. *Galveston Daily News*, "Chop Suey," October 15, 1922, http://access. newspaperarchive.com/galveston-daily-news/1922-10-15   (accessed December 15, 2013).

172. Chalfant, *Galveston*, 26–27.

173. *Galveston Daily News*, "Brock Sisters, Direct from Chicago Night Club, Will Open at Hollywood," June 7, 1926, http://access.newspaperarchive. com/galveston-daily-news/1926-06-07 (accessed September 28, 2013); U.S. Bureau of Labor, "Statistics."

174. *Galveston Daily News*, "Dinner Club Near Completion," May 16, 1926, http://access.newspaperarchive.com/galveston-daily-news/1926-05-16 (accessed December 12, 2013).

175. Cartwright, *Galveston*, 214–15; Nieman, "Galveston's Balinese Room."

176. Chalfant, *Island of Chance*, 28.

177. *Portsmouth Times*, "Ex-Barber Runs Plushy Game Room in Texas," April 23, 1947, http://access.newspaperarchive.com/portsmouth-times/1947-04-23 (accessed October 3, 2013).

178. Nieman, "Galveston's Balinese Room."

179. *Galveston Daily News*, "Hollywood Club to Have Gate Opening," June 8, 1926, http://access.newspaperarchive.com/galveston-daily-news/1926-06-08 (accessed September 26, 2013).

180. *Galveston Daily News*, "Big Time Talent Booked for Club," June 2, 1926, http://access.newspaperarchive.com/galveston-daily-news/1926-06-02 (accessed September 26, 2013).

181. *Galveston Daily News*, "Hollywood Dinner Club Engages Harry Samuels Dance Orchestra from Dallas," May 30, 1926, http://access.newspaperarchive.com/galveston-daily-news/1926-05-30 (accessed September 3, 2013).

182. *Dallas Morning News*, "Asks Forfeiture of Charter of Hollywood Club at Galveston," August 19, 1927, http://access.newspaperarchive.com/dallas-morning-news/1927-08-19 (accessed September 30, 2013).

183. *Galveston Daily News*, "In Nightlife Hey Day Burned Club Was Gulf Gaming Mecca," August 13, 1959, http://access.newspaperarchive.com/galveston-daily-news/1959-08-13 (accessed September 15, 2013).

184. *Galveston Daily News*, "Night Club Faces Contempt Citation: Pollard Files Motion Asking Action Be Taken against Hollywood," August 19, 1927, http://access.newspaperarchive.com/galveston-daily-news/1927-08-19 (accessed September 13, 2013).

185. *Galveston Daily News*, "Crescent City Boy Bears Good Record: Four Preliminary Bouts to Support Main Fight," December 15, 1933, http://access.newspaperarchive.com/galveston-daily-news/1933-12-15 (accessed October 3, 2013).

186. *Dallas Morning News*, "Sam Maceo, Galveston Figure, Dies," April 17, 1951, www.genealogybank.com (accessed October 7, 2013).

187. *Galveston County Daily News*, "More about Galveston's Past," September 7, 1997, http://access.newspaperarchive.com/galveston-county-daily-news/1997-09-07 (assessed August 2, 2013); *Dallas Morning News*, "Lombardo Band Opens in Galveston April 18," April 15, 1934, http://access.newspaperarchive.com/dallas-morning-news/1934-04-15 (accessed July 12, 2013).

188. *Dallas Morning News*, "Talent Added to Hollywood Club Program: Ben Bernie to Remain for Three More Weeks in Dance Rendezvous," August 12, 1934, http://access.newspaperarchive.com/dallas-morning-news/1934-08-12 (accessed October 9, 2013).

189. *Dallas Morning News*, "Arnheim for Dallas," November, 23 1934, http://access.newspaperarchive.com/dallas-morning-news/1934-11-23 (accessed October 9, 1934).

190. Nieman, "Galveston's Balinese Room," 6.

191. *Galveston County Daily News*, N. Ferre, "Balinese Room was Symbol of Old-Time Galveston," January 1, 2009, http://access. newspaperarchive.com/galveston-county-daily-news/2009-01-01 (accessed June 13, 2013).

192. *Galveston County Daily News*, William Cherry, "How the Maceos Created the Balinese Room," July 13, 2003, http://access. newspaperarchive.com/galveston-county-daily-news/2003-07-13 (accessed July 01, 2013).

193. Ibid.

194. Ibid.

195. Nieman, "Galveston's Balinese Room," 7; Cartwright, *Galveston*, 41–44.

196. Nieman, "Galveston's Balinese Room," 9–10.

197. Cartwright, "One Last Shot."

198. Burka, "Grande Dame."

199. Cherry, "How the Maceos Created the Balinese Room."

200. Sam A. Maceo, "Guest Column," *Galveston Daily News*, August 2, 2007, http://access. newspaperarchives.com/galveston-daily-news/2007-08-02 (accessed September 10, 2013).

201. Nieman, "Galveston's Balinese Room," 8.

202. Cartwright, "One Last Shot."

203. Llewellyn, "Good Samaritan," 5.

204. William Cherry, "Happy Birthday to George Mitchell," *Galveston County Daily News*, May 21, 2004, http://access.newspaperarchive.com/galveston-daily-news/2004-05-21 (accessed October 10, 2013).

205. Maceo, "Guest Column."

206. T.E. Bell, "Sin City Revisited," *Houston Chronicle*, November 23, 1986, http://access.newspaperarchive.com/houston-chronicle/1986-11-23 (accessed October 28, 2013).

207. Brown, *Free Rein*, 36–45.

208. Nieman, "Galveston's Balinese Room," 10.

209. Carla Gillogly-Torres,"Strand Theatre Readies for Epic Tale of Island History," *Galveston Daily News*, June 29, 2003, http://access. newspaperarchive.com/galveston-daily-news/2003-06-26 (accessed November 13, 2013).

210. Cartwright, "One Last Shot."

CHAPTER 5

211. Stephen Davis, "James V. Allred and the Texas Governor's Race of 1936," April 28, 1983, James V. Allred Collection, Special Collections, University of Houston Libraries, Houston, TX.

212. "Mr. Johnson" to James V. Allred, February 8, 1934, Allred Collection.

213. "A Citizen Who Stands For Law Enforcement" to Allred, February 28, 1934, Allred Collection.

214. Reverend Charles D. Snowden to Allred August 25, 1936, Allred Collection.

215. R.A. Kemp to Allred, April 4, 1938, Allred Collection.

216. "Citizen for Law Enforcement" to Allred, February 28, 1934, Allred Collection.

217. "Galveston's Merry-Go-Round," *Texas World* (undated clipping), Allred Collection.

218. L.G. Phares to Allred, January 6, 1936, Allred Collection.

219. Cabot, "Lust and Marijuana," 4–13.

220. " *Galveston Daily News*, "Death of Houstonian Believed Underworld's Penalty for Informing," February 27, 1932, http://access. newspaperarchive.com/galveston-daily-news/1932-02-27 (accessed March 4, 2014).

221. *Dallas Morning News*, "Maceo: Removal Decision Due Monday," January 22, 1938, http://www. genealogybank.com (accessed October 7, 2013).

222. Cabot, "Lust and Marijuana," 4–13.

223. Ibid.

224. *Mexia Weekly Herald*, "Large Bond Is Set for Maceo and Nine More," October 8, 1937, 2013, http://texashistory.unt.edu (accessed September 12).

225. *Times-Picayune*, "Double of Maceo Is Introduced at Narcotic Hearing," October 20, 1937, http://www. genealogybank.com (accessed October 8, 2013).

226. *Dallas Morning News*, "Narcotic Agent Heard at Maceo Removal Hearing," January 21, 1938, http://www.genealogybank.com (accessed October 8, 2013).

227. *Heraldo de Brownsville*, "Commissioner Will Decide Maceo Fate," January 23, 1938, http://www. genealogy.com (accessed October 8, 2013).

228. *Dallas Morning News*, "Phil Harris Testifies for Sam Maceo," October 2, 1942, http://www.genealogy. com (accessed October 7, 2013).

229. *Mexia Weekly Herald*, "Large Bond." The Harrison Act, also known as the Harrison Narcotics Tax Act, was approved in 1914. This federal legislation was used to regulate and tax the production, importation and distribution of opiate drugs.

230. *Dallas Morning News*, "Maceo's Hearing on Dope Charges May Be Held Here," December 19, 1937, http://www.genealogybank.com (accessed October 8, 2013).

231. *Times-Picayune*, "Double of Maceo."

232. *Heraldo de Brownsville*, "Maceo: Fights U.S. Charges: Hot Spot Owner Balks at Removal Order," January 10, 1938, http://www.genealogybank.com (accessed October 7, 1938).

233. *Dallas Morning News*, "Narcotics Agent Heard."

234. *Dallas Morning News*, "Maceo: Files Suit to Block His Removal East," January 25, 1938, http://www. genealogybank.com (accessed October 8, 2013).

235. *St. Petersburg Times*, "Texas: Gambling Lords," October 13, 1950, http://www.genealogybank.com (accessed October 3, 2013).

236. *Dallas Morning News*, "Maceo: Files Suit."

237. *Dallas Morning News*, "Maceo: Loses Again, Must Face New York Trial," January 30, 1938, http://www.genealogybank.com (accessed October 7, 2013).

238. *Borger Daily Herald*, "Court Upholds Maceo Decision," July 22, 1938, http://texashistory.unt.edu (accessed September 12, 2013).

239. *Dallas Morning News*, "Maceo: Vainly Fights Removal for Drug Trial: Galvestonian's Appeal Fails to Kill Issue of Probable Cause," July 23, 1938, http://www. genealogybank.com (accessed October 7, 2013).

240. *Sweetwater Reporter*, "Bond Denied to Dope Suspect," August 26, 1938, http://texashistory.unt.edu (accessed September 12, 2013).

241. *San Antonio Light*, "Maceo: Ready to Leave for N.Y. Trial," August 28, 1938, http://access.newspaperarchive.com/san-antonio-light/1938-08-28 (accessed October 11, 2013).

242. *Borger Daily Herald*, "Maceo: Pleads Innocent to Narcotics Charge," August 30, 1938, http://texashistory.unt.edu (accessed September 12, 2013).

243. *Corpus Christi Times*, "Judge at Houston Sentences 9 People in Narcotics Case," October 21, 1938, http://access.newspaperarchive.com/corpus-christi-times/1938-10-21 (accessed March 3, 2014).

244. *Galveston Daily News*, "Delay is Seen in Trial of Maceo," February 10, 1939, http://access.newspaperarchive.com/galveston-daily-news/1939-02-10 (accessed March 3, 2014).

245. *Galveston Daily News*, "15 Indicted at New Orleans in Dope Case," January 21, 1939, http://access.newspaperarchives.com/galveston-daily-news/1939-01-21 (accessed March 5, 2014).

246. *Galveston Daily News*, "Delay Is Seen."

247. *San Antonio Light,* "Near Decision on Maceo Case," May 16, 1939, http://access.newspaperarchive.com/san-antonio-light/1939-05-16 (accessed March 2, 2014).

248. *Galveston Daily News,* "Supreme Court to Act in New York Narcotic Case," October 8, 1939, http://access.newspaperarchive.com/galveston-daily-news/1939-10-08 (accessed March 3, 2014).

249. *Corsicana Daily Sun,* "Trial of Sam Maceo Is Held in Abeyance," October, 17, 1939, http://access. newspaperarchivecom/Corsicana-daily-sun/1939-10-17 (accessed March 3, 2014).

250. *San Antonio Express,* "Sam Maceo Indictment Removed from Calendar," September 5, 1940, http://access.newspaperarchive.com/san-antonio-express/1940-09-05 (accessed March 5, 2014).

251. *Daily Court Review,* "Woman Named Prosecutor."

252. *Brownsville Herald,* "Night Club Operator Faces Federal Trail," August 3, 1942, http://access. newspaperarchive.com/Brownsville-herald/1942-08-03 (accessed March 6, 2014).

253. *Dallas Morning News,* "Maceo: Called Drug Peddler, Fine Citizen: Prosecution, Defense Give Statements as Texan's Trial Opens," September 23, 1942, http://www.genealogybank.com (accessed October 7, 2013); *Milwaukee Journal,* "Navy Lieutenant Tells of Finding Dope Ring," September 28, 1942, http://www.genealogybank.com (accessed October 3, 2013).

254. *Galveston Daily News,* "Narcotic Case to Be Resumed Today," October 18, 1937, http://access.newspaperarchive.com/galveston-daily-news/1937-10-18 (accessed March 4, 2014).

255. *Milwaukee Journal,* "Navy Lieutenant Tells."

256. Ibid.

257. *Galveston Daily News,* "Narcotic Money Said Exchanged at Maceo's Club: Katherine Phillips Says Defendant Was 'Personal Friend,'" October 6, 1942, http://access.newspaperarchive.com/galveston-daily-news/1942-10-06 (accessed March 5, 2014).

258. *Times-Picayune,* "Orchestra Head Maceo Witness at Gotham Trial: Phil Harris Aids Alibi; Tells of Party for Weiss in Texas," October 3, 1942, http://www.genealogybank.com (accessed October 8, 2013).

259. *Galveston Daily News,* "Narcotic Money."

260. *Dallas Morning News,* "Maceo's Jury Fails to Agree," October 24, 1942, http://www.genealogybank. com (accessed October 8, 2013).

261. *Pittsburgh Press,* "Politician Freed of Dope Charges," October 24, 1942, http://www.genealogybank. com (accessed October 3, 2013).

262. *Mexia Weekly Herald,* "Large Bond."

263. *St. Petersburg Times*, "Texas: Gambling Lords,"

264. Nieman, "Galveston's Balinese Room," 16.

265. Gooding and Nieman, *Ed Gooding*, 111; Nieman, "Galveston's Balinese Room," 16.

266. McComb, *Galveston*, 40–56.

267. Cheryl Coggins Frink, "High-Stakes Entertainment," *Austin American-Statesman*, March 2, 1986.

268. Kim Hogstrom, "Galveston! The Musical."

269. Brady Mahoney, "Discovering Our History: Galveston: The Maceo Empire," *Baywatcher*, undated clipping, Galveston and Texas History Center, Rosenberg Library.

270. Nieman, "Galveston's Balinese Room," 12.

271. Remmers, *Going Down the Line*, 24.

272. Ibid.

273. Nieman, "Galveston's Balinese Room," 11.

CHAPTER 6

274. Reppetto, *American Mafia*, 6–7.

275. United States Senate, *Final Report*.

276. Denton and Morris, *Money and Power*, 38–49.

277. Newton, *Mr. Mob*, 40–41.

278. Russo, *Supermob*, 205–06.

279. Rothman, *Neon Metropolis*, 13.

280. United States Senate, *Final Report*.

281. Russo, *Supermob*, 205–06.

282. Denton and Morris, *Money and Power*, 38–49.

283. Ibid.; Russo, *Supermob*, 205–06.

284. Rothman, *Neon Metropolis*, 13–15.

285. *Free Lance-Star*, "Sam Maceo Dies After Operation," April 17, 1951, http://www.genealogybank.com (accessed October 3, 2013).

286. *Dallas Morning News*, "Sam Maceo's Body Brought to Texas," April 18, 1951, http://www. genealogybank.com (accessed October 8, 2013).

287. *Dallas Morning News*, "Maceo: Taking 2-Month Trip," August 1, 1951, http://www.genealogybank.com (accessed October 7, 2013).

288. *Corpus Christi Times*, "Island Gaming Kingpin Rose Maceo Dies," March 15, 1954, http://access. newspaperarchive.com/corpus-christi-times/1954-03-15 (accessed October 7, 2013).

289. *Dallas Morning News*, "Sam Maceo, Galveston Figure, Dies," April 17, 1951, http://www. genealogybank.com (accessed October 7, 2013).

290. Brady Mahoney, "Discovering Our History: Galveston: The Maceo Empire," *Baywatcher*, undated clipping, Galveston and Texas History Center, Rosenberg Library.

291. Nieman, "Galveston's Balinese Room," 11.

292. *Baytown Sun*, "Court Chops Bookies' Phone Lines: Daniel Suit Charges Bell, SW Associated Aided Maceo Mob," June 7, 1951, http://access. newspaperarchive. com/baytown-sun/1951-06-07 (accessed March 21, 2014).

293. *Galveston Daily News*, "State Knocks Out Race Service: Officials Plan Cooperation," June 8, 1951, http://access.newspaperarchive.com/ galveston-daily-news/1951-06-08 (accessed March 20, 2014).

294. *Baytown Sun*, "Court Chops Lines."

295. Ibid.

296. *Galveston Daily News*, "State Knocks Out."

297. Nieman, "Galveston's Balinese Room," 11.

298. Brown, *Free Rein*, 115–20.

299. Nieman, "Galveston's Balinese Room," 11.

300. Brown, *Free Rein*, 115–20.

301. "Wide-Open Galveston."

302. Terry Macleod, "Fertitta Fined $25 on Assault Charge," *Galveston Daily News*, August 9, 1955, http://access.newspaperarchive.com/galveston-daily-news/1955-08-09 (accessed March 1, 2014).

303. Ibid.

304. "Wide-Open Galveston."

305. Nieman, "Galveston's Balinese Room," 12.

306. Ibid.

307. Ibid.

308. George Belk, "More Gaming Units Seized in Crackdown," *Galveston Daily News*, June 19, 1957, http://access.newspaperarchive.com/ galveston-daily-news/1957-06-19 (accessed March 15, 2014).

309. Gooding and Nieman, *Ed Gooding*, 113–15.

310. Ibid.

311. *Galveston Daily News*, "Balinese Room to Have Third 'Sold Out' House," June 14, 1958, 2014, http://access.newspaperarchive.com/galveston-daily-news/1958-06-14 (accessed March 15).

312. Barry Hart, "More Indictments Returned: 16 for Gambling Violations," *Galveston Daily News*, September 27, 1957, http://access.newspaperarchive. com/galveston-daily-news/1957-09-27 (accessed March 15, 2014).

313. Stanley Babb, "Suspended Sentence in Gaming Trial: A. Fertitta Guilty on One Count," *Galveston Daily News*, April 17, 1959, http://access. newspaperarchive.com/galveston-daily-news/1959-04-17 (accessed March 15, 2014).

314. Brown, *Free Rein*, 119.

315. Steve McGonigle, "How $100M Turns into $516K," *Dallas Morning News*, May 13, 2012, http://www. dallasnews.com/archives (accessed June 6, 2013).

316. Balboni, *Beyond the Mafia*, 32–33.

317. *Madison Wisconsin State Journal*, "Jurors Hear Secret FBI Tapes of Game-Skimming Methods," December 5, 1985, http://access.newspaperarchive. com/madison-wisconsin-state-journal/1985-12-5 (accessed March 2, 2014).

318. Balboni, *Beyond the Mafia*, 32–33.

319. Ibid.

320. Ibid.

321. Oskar Garcia, "Frank Fertitta Jr., Founder of Station Casinos; at 70," *Boston Globe*, August 24, 2009, http://www.boston.com/search/archives_ subscriber_note/ (accessed June 10, 2013).

322. *USA Today*, "'Whitey' Bulger Arrest."

CHAPTER 7

323. Drew Pearson, "Personal and Political Risk for Kefauver in His Probe," *St. Petersburg Times*, October 13, 1950, http://news.google.com/ newspapers (accessed January 2, 2014).

324. *Galveston Daily News*, "Miller's Isle: Houston Newsman-Author Takes a Look at Galveston—Past, Present, and Future," November 6, 1983, http://access.newspaperarchive.com/galveston-daily-news/1983-1-06 (accessed October 6, 2013).

BIBLIOGRAPHY

PRIMARY SOURCES

Archives

Allred, James V. Collection. Special Collections. University of Houston Library. Houston, TX.

United States Bureau of the Census. "Fifteenth Census, 1930." Record Group 29. National Archives, Washington, D.C. www.ancestry.com (accessed September 5, 2013).

———. "Fourteenth Census, 1920." Record Group 29. National Archives, Washington, D.C. www.ancestry.com.

———. "Thirteenth Census, 1910." Record Group 29. National Archives, Washington, D.C. www.ancestry.com (accessed September 9, 2013).

———. "2008–2012 American Community Survey." http://factfinder2.census.gov/ (accessed January 30, 2014).

———. "2010 Census Report." http://quickfacts.census.gov/qfd/states/48/48167.html (accessed June 3, 2013).

United States Bureau of Labor. "Statistics, Databases, Tables, and Calculators by Subject, CPI Inflation Calculator." http://www.bls.gov/data/inflation_calculator.htm (accessed October 27, 2013).

United States Congress. Senate. *Final Report of the Special Senate Committee to Investigate Organized Crime in Interstate Commerce.* 82nd Cong., 1951. S. Doc. 725. http://www.nevadaobserver.com/Reading%20Room%20 Documents/Kefauver%20Final%20Report.htm (accessed June 13, 2013).

BIBLIOGRAPHY

United States Customs Service. "Passenger Lists of Vessels Arriving at New Orleans, Louisiana, 1903–1945." Record Group 36. National Archives, Washington, D.C. www.ancestry.com (accessed September 5, 2013).

United States Department of War. "World War I Draft Registration Cards, 1917–1918, Galveston County, Texas." Record Group 163. National Archives, Washington, D.C. www.ancestry.com (accessed September 8, 2013).

Newspapers

Austin American Statesman
Baytown (TX) Sun
Borger (TX) Daily Herald
Boston Globe
Brownsville (TX) Herald
Corpus Christi (TX) Times
Corsicana (TX) Daily Sun
Dallas Morning News
Fort Worth Star-Telegram
Fredericksburg (VA) Free Lance-Star
Galveston Baywatcher
Galveston County Daily News
Galveston Daily News
Galveston Tribune
Heraldo de Brownsville (TX)

Houston Chronicle
Lubbock (TX) Morning Avalanche
Madison (WI) Daily Journal
Mexia (TX) Weekly Herald
Milwaukee Journal
New Orleans Times-Picayune
Orange (TX) Leader
Pittsburgh (PA) Press
Port Arthur (TX) News
Portsmouth (OH) Times
San Antonio Express
San Antonio Light
St. Petersburg (FL) Times
Sweetwater (TX) Reporter
Victoria Advocate

SECONDARY SOURCES

Periodicals

Burka, Paul. "Grande Dame of the Gulf." Texas Monthly, December 1983. http://www.texasmonthly.com/ content/grande-dame-gulf (accessed June 16, 2013).

Cabot, Heloise. "A Lesson in Lust and Marijuana: Weed of Sin!" American Detective, 1938.

Cartwright, Gary. "One Last Shot." Texas Monthly, June 1993. http://www.texasmonthly.com/story/one-last-shot/page/0/3 (accessed June 3, 2013).

Daily Court Review. "Woman Named Prosecutor in Sam Maceo Case." April 29, 1942. access.newspaperarchive. com/daily-court-review/ 1942-04-29 (accessed March 5, 2014).

Hogstrom, Kim. "Galveston! The Musical Tells Maceo Brothers' Story." Your Houston News, September 28, 2011. http://www.yourhoustonnews. com/greater_houston/entertainment/galveston-themusical-tells-maceo-brothers-story/article_61839a93-06d6-5434-8c9e-907e88131cb1.html (accessed October 4, 2013).

Llewellyn, Edwin E. "A Good Samaritan Has Passed On." *Galveston Isle: The Magazine of Galveston, Texas*, 1951.

Nieman, Robert. "Galveston's Balinese Room: Born: 1942–Died 2008." *Texas Ranger Dispatch* 27 (2008). http://www.texasranger.org/dispatch/Backissues/Dispatch_Issue_27.pdf (accessed June 24, 2013).

Scarpaci, Jean Ann. "Immigrants in the New South: Italians in Louisiana's Sugar Parishes, 1810–1910." *Labor History* 16 (1975).

Shanabruch, Charles. "The Louisiana Immigration Movement, 1891–1907: An Analysis of Efforts, Attitudes, and Opportunities." *Louisiana History: The Journal of the Louisiana Historical Association* 18 (1977).

USA Today. "Whitey Bulger Arrest Recalls UFC Owner's Roots." June 23, 2011. usatoday30.usatoday.com/sports/mma/post/2011/06/whitey-bulger-capture-recalls-zuffa-roots (accessed June 2, 2013).

"Wide-Open Galveston Mocks Texas Law." *Life*, August 15, 1955. http://books.google.com/books/about/LIFE.html?id=51YEAAAAMBAJ (accessed June 2, 2013).

Books

Balboni, Alan Richard. *Beyond the Mafia: Italian Americans and the Development of Las Vegas*. Reno: University of Nevada Press, 1996.

Barnstone, Howard. *The Galveston That Was*. New York: MacMillan Company, 1963.

Beales, Derek. *The Risorgimento and the Unification of Italy*. London: George Allen & Unwin, 1971.

Bixel, Patricia Bellis, and Elizabeth Hayes Turner. *Galveston and the 1900 Storm: Catastrophe and Catalyst*. Austin: University of Texas Press, 2000.

Blocker, Jack S., David M. Fahey and Ian R. Tyrrell. *Alcohol and Temperance in Modern History: An International Encyclopedia*. Vol. 1. Santa Barbara, CA: ABC-CLIO, 2003.

Brown, Jean M. *Free Rein: Galveston Island's Alcohol, Gambling, and Prostitution Era, 1839–1957*. Beaumont, TX: Lamar University, 1998.

Cartwright, Gary. *Galveston: A History of the Island*. New York: MacMillan Publishing Company, 1991.

Chalfant, Frank E. *Galveston: Island of Chance*. Houston: Treasures of Nostalgia, 1997.

Clark, Martin. *The Italian Risorgimento*. London: Pearson Education Limited, 1998.

Collins, Ace. *Tragedies of American History: 13 Stories of Human Error and Natural Disasters*. New York: Penguin Group, 2003.

BIBLIOGRAPHY

Denton, Sally, and Roger Morris. *The Money and the Power: The Making of Las Vegas and Its Hold on America, 1947–2000.* New York: Random House, 2002.

Dickie, John. *Cosa Nostra: A History of the Sicilian Mafia.* New York: Palgrave McMillan, 2004.

Gooding, Ed, and Robert Nieman. *Ed Gooding: Soldier, Texas Ranger.* Longview, TX: Ranger Publishing, 2001.

Green, Nathan C. *Story of the 1900 Galveston Hurricane.* New Orleans: Pelican Publishing Company, 2000.

Hardwick, Susan Wiley. *Mythic Galveston: Reinventing America's Third Coast.* Baltimore: Johns Hopkins University Press, 2002.

Hayes, Charles W. *Galveston: History of the Island and the City.* Vol. 1. Austin, TX: Jenkins Garrett Press, 1974.

Humble, Ronald. *Frank Nitti: The True Story of Chicago's Notorious "Enforcer."* Fort Lee, NJ: Barricade Books, 2008.

Larson, Erik. *Isaac's Storm: A Man, a Time, and the Deadliest Hurricane in History.* New York: Vintage Books, 2000.

Mallory, Stephen L. *Understanding Organized Crime.* Boston: Jones & Bartlett Learning, 2012.

Marinbach, Bernard. *Galveston: Ellis Island of the West.* Albany: State University of New York Press, 1983.

McComb, David G. *Galveston: A History.* Austin: University of Texas Press, 1986.

Newton, Michael. *Mr. Mob: The Life and Crimes of Moe Dalitz.* West Jefferson, NC: McFarland & Company, 2007.

Remmers, Mary W. *Going Down the Line: Galveston's Red-Light District Remembered.* Galveston, TX: privately published, 1997.

———. *Portrait of Galveston Island: 1300 Years of the City's History A.D. 700/800– 2000.* Galveston, TX: privately published, 2002.

Repetto, Thomas. *American Mafia: A History of Its Rise to Power.* New York: Henry Holt and Company, 2004.

Rothman, Hal. *Neon Metropolis: How Las Vegas Started the Twenty-first Century.* New York: Routledge, 2003.

Russo, Gus. *Supermob: How Sidney Korshak and His Criminal Associates Became America's Hidden Power Brokers.* New York: Bloomsbury, 2006.

Saladino, Salvatore. *Italy from Unification to 1919: Growth and Decay of a Liberal Regime.* New York: Thomas Y. Crowell Company, 1970.

Tyler, Ron, et al., eds. *The New Handbook of Texas.* 6 vols. Austin: Texas State Historical Association, 1996. http://www.tshaonline.org/handbook/online/articles/bmk05.

Young, Earle B. *Galveston and the Great West.* College Station: Texas A&M University Press, 1997.

INDEX

INDEX

INDEX

INDEX

INDEX

ABOUT THE AUTHORS

SCOTT H. BELSHAW

Dr. Scott Belshaw holds a PhD in juvenile justice from Prairie View A&M University, a member of the Texas A&M University System. He earned his bachelor of science in social sciences and psychology from the University of Houston. He also holds both a master of liberal arts from Houston Baptist University and a master of arts in criminology from the University of Houston–Clear Lake. His PhD dissertation examined sexually abused women in the juvenile justice system. His dissertation research has been cited and used by numerous advocacy groups and organizations.

Dr. Belshaw is currently an assistant professor (tenure track) of criminal justice at the University of North Texas. He also served as an adjunct professor of forensic psychology at Argosy University in the Dallas area and has taught undergraduate and graduate courses in criminal justice and psychology.

Dr. Belshaw has published research in numerous academic journals such as *Criminal Justice Review*, *Criminal Justice Policy Review*, *Journal of Criminal Justice Education*, *American Journal of Criminal Justice*, *International Journal of Punishment and Sentencing*, *Southwestern Journal of Criminal Justice* and numerous other educational and criminal justice–related journals.

Dr. Belshaw is also a veteran of the United States Navy and Naval Reserve and served during Operation Desert Storm.

ABOUT THE AUTHORS

RICHARD B. MCCASLIN

Dr. Richard B. McCaslin chairs the Department of History at the University of North Texas. His *Lee in the Shadow of Washington* was nominated for a Pulitzer Prize, and it won a Laney Prize from the Austin Civil War Round Table and the Slatten Award from the Virginia Historical Society. *Tainted Breeze: The Great Hanging at Gainesville, Texas, October 1862* earned the Tullis Prize from the Texas State Historical Association and a commendation from the Association for State and Local History. *At the Heart of Texas: One Hundred Years of the Texas State Historical Association, 1897–1997* received the Award of Merit from the Texas Philosophical Society. Most recently, *Fighting Stock: John S. "Rip" Ford in Texas* won the Pate Award from the Fort Worth Civil War Round Table and the Bates Award from the Texas State Historical Association. He is a fellow of the Texas State Historical Association.

T. NICOLE BOATMAN

Nicole Boatman earned her bachelor of science in psychology from the University of North Texas in 2012. Upon completion of her degree, Nicole went on to work in the private sector of behavioral health for one of the largest healthcare management companies in the country. She returned to UNT to work as a teaching assistant and complete her master of science in criminal justice. Her thesis provided a historical account of Texas organized crime, which led to the development of this project. Since graduating, she has been working as an investigator for one of the nation's largest customer-oriented private investigation firms.

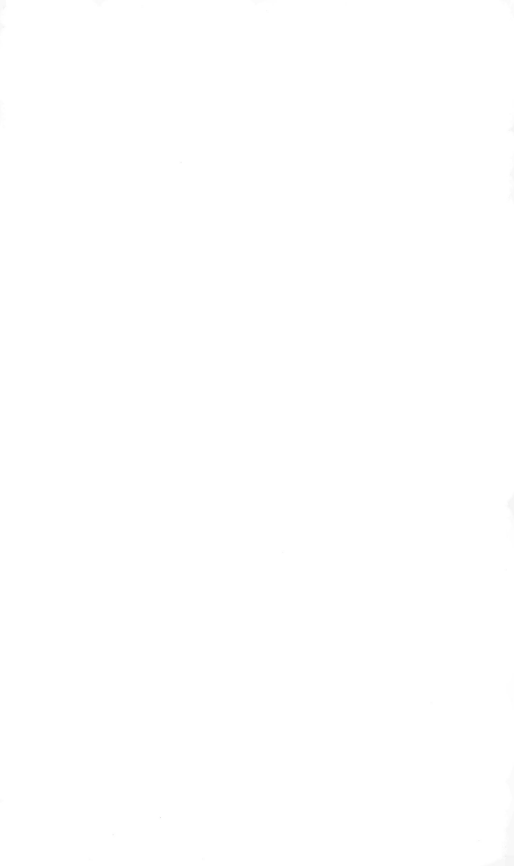

CPSIA information can be obtained
at www.ICGtesting.com
Printed in the USA
LVHW011115141222
735207LV00008B/36